P9-DEZ-447

ALSO BY JOE QUEENAN

Imperial Caddy

If You're Talking to Me, Your Career Must Be in Trouble

The Unkindest Cut

RED LOBSTER
WHITE TRASH
and The
BLUE LAGOON

Joe Queenan's America

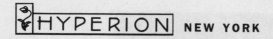 HYPERION NEW YORK

The introduction and portions of Chapters 1, 3, 5, and 7 have appeared in different form in *GQ*, *Playboy*, and *TV Guide*.

Designed by Helene Wald Berinsky

Library of Congress Cataloging-In-Publication Data
Queenan, Joe.
    Red lobster, white trash, and the blue lagoon : Joe Queenan's
America / Joe Queenan.—1st ed.
        p. cm.
     ISBN 0-7868-6332-3
     1. Popular culture—United States—History—20th century.
    2. United States—Social life and customs—1971–   3. Queenan, Joe.
    I. Title.
    E169.04.Q44   1998
    306 0973—dc21   98-10821
                                                                    CIP

FIRST EDITION

10   9   8   7

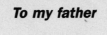

To my father

ACKNOWLEDGMENTS

The author wishes to thank Jennifer Barth, editor; Joe Vallely, agent; Martin Beiser, colleague; and Gino Salomone, consigliere.

CONTENTS

Introduction: How Bad Could It Be?   1

1. Slouching Toward Red Lobster   5

2. The Satanic Verses   21

3. The Howling   39

4. Only the Good Die Young   61

5. The Mistake by the Lake   79

6. Iowa on the Hudson   93

7. Touched by a Devil   113

8. French Leave   127

9. Into the Mystic   139

10. He Wore Blue Velvet   157

11. Deliverance   175

    Index   189

INTRODUCTION:
HOW BAD COULD IT BE?

When I was coming of age in the late 1960s, most of my generation was involved in a heroic effort to depose Bob Hope, John Wayne, Lawrence Welk, Sammy Davis, Jr., and all the other cultural icons who ruled American society with an iron fist. This was an intellectual insurrection from which I defected by my twenty-first birthday. One reason I threw in the towel so quickly was because I recognized almost immediately that Cat Stevens and Iron Butterfly were not all that much of an improvement over Shecky Greene and Liberace.

But even more central to my decision to cut and run was the glum recognition that mainstream American culture is too daunting an enemy to fight. American pop culture comes at you in waves, so even if you do manage to fend off "Gilligan's Island," "Ironside," and Loggins & Messina, you'll still have to reckon with "The Partridge Family," "The Brady Bunch," and Seals & Crofts. To paraphrase the old "pony soldiers multiply like the blades of grass" chestnut, for every

Tony Orlando that you polish off, ten Tony Danzas will spring up in his place.

Ever since that watershed moment in my youth, I meekly accepted the fact that this society was dominated by the likes of William Shatner, not William Shakespeare, and that it was basically designed for the greater glory of Richard Simmons, not Richard Thompson, and certainly not Richard Strauss. In short, I made a separate peace. I staked out a tiny corner that I could call my own, where I amused myself for the next twenty-five years, listening to Elvis Costello and Igor Stravinsky, reading Tom McGuane and Henry James novels, watching Satyajit Ray and Gary Oldman movies, fully aware that I was but a guest in the Empire of the Sonny Bono.

I can say, without a trace of bitterness, that throughout this period I was both touched and gratified by the indulgence that my fellow Americans manifested toward me during this long sojourn in the cultural wilderness we call home. If this were a truly bad country, my neighbors would have killed me off long ago. Instead, for most of my adult life they merely rolled their eyes and chided me for my puzzling failure to buy Robert Ludlum novels, watch "America's Funniest Home Videos," or occasionally hum a tune from *Les Miz*. They always found me odd. They did not find me evil.

But by March 1996, at the age of forty-five, I found myself growing weary of the elite, effete subculture that I had for so long occupied. Reading *The New Republic* every week had turned into an irksome chore. Seeing Placido Domingo at the Met had become a big yawn. Endless dinner conversations with friends about the camera angles in *Jean de Florette* and the use of incongruous terms such as "force majeure" in Coen Brothers films had lost their appeal. At some level of my subconscious, a certain fatigue had set in. Perhaps I yearned for something entirely different. Or perhaps, for the first time in my life, I was beginning to suspect that snobs like me were cutting ourselves off from all the fun in this society, that in our obsession with books by Umberto Eco and concerts by the Kronos Quartet, we had deprived ourselves of the boundless joy to be derived from a quiet evening with Yanni.

After many weeks of burgeoning ennui, I arrived at a crucial decision. For the first time in my life, I would throw off the mask of the urbane sophisticate and plunge headfirst into the culture of the masses, setting aside my haughty pretensions and drowning myself in the hurly-burly world of the hoi polloi. For the next few weeks, I would furlough that part of my brain that had long revered the rare, precious, and beautiful, and instead zero in on the hopelessly plebian. I would eat at the kinds of restaurants that never made the *Zagat Survey*. I would attend the kinds of musicals where the bomber jackets they sold in the lobby were more interesting than the cast. I would read the kinds of books that chunky men on their way to important meetings in Knoxville, Tennessee, always seemed to be reading in the La Guardia Airport departure lounge. I would rent the kinds of movies that chunky men watched on pay-per-view when their important meetings in Knoxville were canceled. And I would listen to the kind of music that my wife could use in divorce proceedings as evidence of child abuse.

I was willing to do all this because I'd had it up to here with the dreary, civilized life I'd been leading. Any change would be for the better. And yes, even if the world I was entering might occasion disappointment, my way of looking at it was:

How bad could it be?

Slouching Toward Red Lobster

*C*ats was very, very, very bad. *Cats* was a lot worse than I'd expected. I'd seen *Phantom* years ago, and knew all I needed to know about *Starlight Express* and *Joseph and the Amazing Technicolor Dreamcoat*, so I was not a complete stranger to the fiendishly vapid world of Andrew Lloyd Webber. But nothing I'd ever read or heard about the show could have prepared me for the epic suckiness of *Cats*. Put it this way: *Phantom* sucked. But *Cats* really sucked.

One of the things that fascinated me about *Cats* was the way I'd managed to keep it from penetrating my consciousness for the previous fourteen years. Yes, I'd been walking past the Winter Garden Theatre at 50th and Broadway since 1982 without once even dreaming of venturing inside; and yes, I'd heard the song "Memory"; and yes, I'd heard about all the Tonys *Cats* had won; and yes, I'd seen all those garish subway posters; and yes, I'd been jostled by those armies of tourists streaming out of the theater at rush hour as I myself tried to hustle through midtown. But all those years that *Cats* had been playing, I'd somehow avoided even finding out what the show was about. Wandering past the Winter Garden all those years was like wandering past those dimly lit S&M bars in Greenwich Village: I really didn't need to know the details.

Now my blissful ignorance had been shattered. So without any further ado, let me share the wealth. For the benefit of the two or three other people in this society who don't know what *Cats* is about, here's the answer: It's about a bunch of cats. The cats jump around in a postnuclear junkyard for some two and a half hours, bumping and grinding to that curiously Mesozoic pop music for which Andrew Lloyd Webber is famous— the kind of full-tilt truckin' that sounds like the theme from "The Mod Squad." There's an Elvis impersonator cat, and a cat that looks like Cyndi Lauper, and a cat that looks like Phyllis Diller. All the other cast members look like Jon Bon Jovi with two weeks of facial growth.

Sure, *Cats* is allegedly based upon the works of T. S. Eliot, but from what I could tell, the show had about as much to do with the author of "The Waste Land" as those old Steve Reeves movies had to do with Euripides. *Cats* is what *Grease* would look like if all the cast members dressed up like KISS. To give you an idea of how bad *Cats* is, think of a musical where you're actually glad to hear "Memory" reprised a third time because all the other songs are so awful. Think of a musical where the songs are so bad that "Memory" starts to sound like "Ol' Man River" by comparison. That's how bad *Cats* is.

The most disappointing thing about my maiden voyage on this sea of sappiness was the behavior of the crowd. In all honesty, I had long assumed that everyone who enjoyed *Cats* was, in some sense of the word, a bozo. But I'd always assumed that they were happy, festive bozos. Nothing could have prepared me for the utterly blasé reception *Cats* received when I attended a matinee in late March. The crowd was your typical Saturday afternoon assemblage: implacable Japanese tourists, platoons of gawking midwestern huckleberries, legions of Farrah Fawcett lookalikes. Based on their fulsome demeanors, I would have expected them to give the performers a boisterous reception when urged to get down and boogie.

But the day I saw *Cats*, the crowd just kind of sat there and zoned out. Not unlike Broadway dancers and singers who sometimes, if not always, phoned it in, the audience was phoning it in. The only way I could rationalize such lack of passion was this: *Cats* had been playing for fourteen years, and this was a room filled with people who had found something better to do with their time for the previous 5,600 performances. So it wasn't like *Cats* was something they'd been dying to see, like the Taj Mahal or the Blarney Stone or that crevice between Sharon Stone's legs. Mostly, they acted like RVers who were simply checking names off a list: "Ohio, New Jersey, Wisconsin—okay, Reba, we've done the Dairy States."

I came home from *Cats* feeling totally dejected. In the back of my mind, I'd expected the show to fall into that vast category occupied by everything from bingo to Benny Hill. You know: so bad, it's good. But *Cats* was just plain bad. Really bad. About as bad as bad could get. Revisiting the horror in my mind later that evening, I consoled myself with the assurance that surely this would be the lowest point of my adventure, that nothing I subsequently experienced could possibly be in even the same league as *Cats*.

Then I cued up the Michael Bolton record.

So much for that theory.

For years, I'd been vaguely aware of Michael Bolton's existence, just as I'd been vaguely aware that there was an ebola virus plague in Africa. Horrible tragedies, yes, but they had nothing to do with me. All that changed when I purchased a copy of *The Classics*. When you work up the gumption to put a record like *The Classics* on your CD player, it's not much different from deliberately inoculating yourself with rabies. With his heart-on-my-sleeve appeals to every emotion no decent human being should even dream of possessing, Michael Bolton is the only person in history who has figured out a way to make "Yesterday" sound worse than the original. He's Mandy Patinkin squared. His sacrilegious version of Sam Cooke's "Bring It on Home to Me" is a premeditated act of cultural ghoulism, a crime of musical genocide tantamount to a Jerry Vale rerecording of the Sex Pistols' "Anarchy in the U.K." And having to sit there and listen while this Kmart Joe Cocker mutilates "You Send Me" is like sitting through a performance of *King Lear* with Don Knotts in the title role. Which leads to the inevitable question: If it's a crime to deface the Statue of Liberty or to spray-paint swastikas on Mount Rushmore or to burn the American flag, why isn't it a crime for Michael Bolton to butcher Irving Berlin's "White Christmas"?

To round out Day One in my personal cultural bathosphere, I picked up Nicholas Evans's international best-seller *The Horse Whisperer*. As was the case with *Cats* and Michael Bolton, the result was horrifying. In Evans's megahyped novel, a tyke loses her leg in a riding accident, then goes out west with her yuppie-scum mother seeking to persuade a sagebrush psychotherapist to cure her totally psychotic horse. With lines like "What wanton liars love makes of us" and "It was the last night of their blinkered idyll," *The Horse Whisperer* is one of those cloying upscale/downscale books where the mom has an attitude, the kid has an attitude, and even the goddamn horse has an attitude.

In fact, the only mildly attractive character in the entire book is Tom Booker, the old horseshit whisperer himself. Booker is a kind of cowpoke philosopher who always knows the right things to whisper into a horse's ears, but seems to have trouble when it comes to whispering into a woman's ears. Maybe that's because horses don't understand the phrase "cornhole." And, oh yes, Tom the Horse Whisperer is *a quiet loner from the great state of Montana.* Of course, I was reading about this ten-gallon, equestophilic Billy Bob Freud right about the time the Unabomber was being brought to justice and the FBI was besieging those madcap Freemen out in the Great State of Montana.

Nice timing, Nicky.

In the days and weeks that followed, I gradually realized that mainstream American culture was infinitely more idiotic than I had ever suspected. Take movies. Over the years, I'd come to believe that a special ring of hell had been reserved for Lorne Michaels for promoting the careers of Joe Piscopo, James Belushi, and others of their ilk. But nothing those dimwits had done on film had even vaguely prepared me for the prepaleolithic world of Adam Sandler and Chris Farley. The whole time I was watching *Billy Madison* and *Tommy Boy* I kept saying to myself, "I know that these people are alumni of 'Saturday Night Live,' so I know that if I sit here long enough, they will eventually do or say something that will make me laugh. Heck, they're pros."

Oh, foolish, foolish man! Hours and hours later, I was still in my chair, comatose, watching these Gen-X Ostrogoths ruin my day, my week, my civilization. Here's Sandler setting a bag of poop on fire. Here's Farley getting covered in cow shit. And here's Bo Derek, co-starring. What a sad commentary on our society that we have produced movies so bad that you feel sorry Bo Derek has to be in them. Which just goes to show: No matter how famous you are when you're young, if you don't play your cards right, you're eventually going to end up in a movie with Adam Sandler.

Was all this a surprise to me? Yes, I can truly say that the scale of horrendousness proudly displayed in these motion pictures was awe-inspiring. Sure, I'd known that these movies were out there, but not until I'd actually sat all the way through a couple of them did I have any idea how satanically cretinous they were. Until I saw *Billy Madison* and *Tommy Boy,* I'd always thought that the three scariest words in the English language were "Starring Dan Aykroyd." Now I knew better. Being introduced to Joe Piscopo and Dan Aykroyd and only later learning of the existence of Adam Sandler and Chris Farley is like going to school and learning about the Black Plague, only to find out many years later that there's something called the Blacker Plague.

And I don't even want to talk about Pauly Shore.

On some of the outings I lined up for my trek through the cultural undergrowth, I honestly suspected that someone had phoned ahead to ensure that the staff would maximize my discomfort. Typical was the night I dragged my family over to the local Red Lobster for our first-ever visit to the garish establishment. Red Lobster, I quickly learned, was a chain geared toward people who think of themselves as just a little bit too upscale for Roy Rogers. Even while waiting in the anteroom of the bogus sea shanty I could detect a certain aura of proletarian snootiness because of the way people were looking at me and my son. While Gordon, age ten, and I had turned up in nondescript T-shirts and shorts, the Red

Lobster patrons were bedecked in their best windbreakers and their very finest polyester trousers.

"Next time, show some respect," their expressions suggested. "After all, you're eating at Red Lobster. This ain't some goddamn Wendy's."

The Red Lobster menu consisted almost entirely of batter cunningly fused with marginally aquatic foodstuffs and configured into clever geometric structures. I immediately began to suspect that the kitchen at Red Lobster consisted of one gigantic vat of grease in which plastic cookie molds resembling various types of food were inserted to create a structural resemblance to the specific item ordered. This was the only way to determine whether you were eating Buffalo wings or crabcakes. Technically, my dinner—The Admiral's Feast—was a dazzling assortment of butterfly shrimp, fish filet, scallops, and some mysterious crablike entity. But in reality, everything tasted exactly like Kentucky Fried Chicken. Even the French fries.

Red Lobster was a consummate bad experience. It wasn't just the Huey Lewis & the News ambience, it wasn't just the absence of mozzarella sticks from the menu that day, it wasn't just the party of twenty-nine seated next to us complaining about the service, it wasn't just the Turtles singing "Happy Together" overhead, it wasn't just the absence of root beer from the menu that day, it wasn't just the titular head of the party of twenty-nine incessantly referring to different members of his entourage as "landlubbers," and it wasn't even the way those social-climbing townies gave my son and me the once-over as we came through the door. No, it was definitely the food. The food tasted like baked, microwaved, reheated, overcooked, deep-fried loin of grease.

Admiral's Feast, my ass.

*   *   *

After my stomach lining had recovered from this dismal gastronomic sortie, I decided to immerse myself further in some of the most beloved books of the past decade. A good place to start was *The Celestine Prophecy*. This enormously popular book deals with the discovery of an ancient manuscript that predicted a revolution in human behavior at the dawn of the next millennium. The manuscript, purportedly written in sixth-century B.C. Aramaic, had been discovered in the rain forests of Peru and contained nine insights. One of the insights involved using a person's psychic energy field to connect with the flora and fauna all around us. The book had sold several million copies, presumably to that unnerving subset of Americans who exercise to Shirley MacLaine videos, are unaware of Dionne Warwick's pre-psychic career, voted for Jerry Brown in the 1992 Democratic primaries, and worship Baal.

I'm as open to suggestions about how to utilize my psychic energy as the next guy, but I do have a few caveats here. For one, I'm getting a bit fed up with the whole Vanquished Chic thing. Basically, anything that has to do with the Hopis, the Etruscans, the Mayans, the Aztecs, or the Incas gets right up my nose for the pure and simple reason that *they lost*. Throughout my life, I've adopted a basic rule of thumb that any wisdom imputed to the denizens of Atlantis, Kathmandu, or Machu Picchu must be viewed with extreme skepticism, because if these folks were so goddamn smart, how come they didn't hang around longer? Look at it this way: Pizarro invades Peru on Sunday, and by Tuesday night he's conquered a nation of 12 million people. How do you lose your entire continent to a couple hundred grungy conquistadors when the odds are that heavily in your favor? The obvious explanation: The Incas were a race of 12 million pre-Columbian Greg Normans.

Gradually, my passion for peerlessly disorienting experiences caused me to experience a strange new emotion. Technically speaking, there is no English phrase or idiom to describe the feeling to which I refer, so here I will take the liberty of coining the term *scheissenbedauern*. This word, which literally means "shit regret," describes the disappointment one feels when exposed to something that is not nearly as bad as one had hoped it would be. A perfect example is Neil Diamond's recent album, *Tennessee Moon*.

"Hollywood don't do what it once could do," Neil sings on the title track, so he packs up his "dusty bags," grabs "an old guitar," and hits "that Blue Highway," rambling back to that "old Tennessee Moon" where he once "fell in love to an old Hank Williams song." Yes, when Neil hears that "lonesome whistle moan," he says, "So long, Big City," because he's "longing for those country roads," and knows it's time to "take a swing down south" to "see if that girl Annie still remembers me."

Let us ignore for a moment the implausible elements in this song, most importantly the fact that Neil Diamond hails from Flatbush. Let us also ignore the fact that The Country Record has been a cliché since Dylan recorded *Nashville Skyline*, that the record contains the obligatory phoned-in Waylon Jennings duet, and that Neil Diamond, a man who makes Burl Ives sound like Joey Ramone, does not come across in an entirely convincing fashion on the John Lee Hooker–type track where he sings "I'm gonna be rockin' tonight." This is a line that reminds me of the time Senator Al

D'Amato got dressed up as "a narc" and went up to Harlem to register a "bust." Man, did some shit go down that day!

Despite this abundant evidence of dire lameness, *Tennessee Moon* did not even approach Michael Bolton's *The Classics* for sheer acreage of horseshit per square foot if only because Neil Diamond at his worst still sounds better than Michael Bolton at his best. The reason? At least Neil wrote the atrocious songs that he was slaughtering.

Yet, much to my consternation, I found this terribly disappointing. At a certain level, I had now begun to hope that everything I encountered would suck in a megasucky way, and was honestly disappointed when some proved merely cruddy. Like Kurtz in *Heart of Darkness*, I wanted to gaze directly into the abyss, to stare at the horror. But as the days passed, as I ventured deeper and deeper into the heartland of hootiness, I grew crestfallen at the failure of certain monstrously popular cultural figures to achieve the bathetic levels I craved. Dean Koontz's *Intensity* was sadistic, depraved, and revolting, but the book could not hold a candle to *The Horse Whisperer*'s Mephistophelian inaneness. *Slam Dunk Ernest,* a direct-to-video film about a lovable moron, was predictably idiotic, but because it had one good joke (Ernest, the unlikely basketball hero, changes his name to Ernest Abdul Mustafa), it could not rival the horrors of *Billy Madison* and *Tommy Boy*.

Garth Brooks—Glen Campbell under an assumed name—was a perfect example of the *scheissenbedauern* phenomenon. Every Garth Brooks song I encountered was a redneck anthem about truckers, drivin' rain, country fairs, burning bridges, that damn old rodeo, ashes on the water. In the typical Brooks song, "Mama's in the graveyard, Papa's in the pen," there's a fire burning bright, "this old highway is like a woman sometimes," and some old cowboy's "heading back from somewhere he never should have been."

Garth is always sayin' a little prayer tonight, payin' his dues, shipping his saddle to Dad. But Jehoshaphat, he wouldn't trade a single day, because love is like a highway, it's one big party, and let's face it: He drew a bull no man could ride. So all that's left to do is whisper a prayer in the fury of the storm and hope you don't miss The Dance.

It goes without saying that folks call Garth a maverick—heck, there "must be rebel blood running through (his) veins." But sometimes you've just got to go against the grain, "buck the system," even though "the deck is stacked against you." In short, Brooks's music was the musical equivalent of a Pat Buchanan stump speech, market-researched baloney where the lyrics were so generic you started to suspect he was using Microsoft's Drugstore Cowboy for Windows 95 (not available in a Macintosh format) to write them.

But even though songs like "We Shall Be Free" blatantly ripped off Sly & the Family Stone—fulfilling the dictum that black music is always ten years ahead of the curve, and country and western twenty years behind it—and even though Brooks recycled more riffs than Ray Davies, and even though Brooks was so bland he made Gordon Lightfoot sound like the Red Hot Chili Peppers, these records didn't actually make you puke. This was about the highest tribute I could pay to most contemporary country-and-western music.

On the other hand, it didn't make me do anything. Somebody once said that when you turn on the radio, Genesis is what comes out. That's exactly the way I felt about Garth Brooks.

So, all right, he chomped, but he didn't chomp royal. He chomped in the same off-the-shelf way most millionaires in hyperthyroid cowboy hats chomped. But he didn't bite the big one. And for some reason, this bothered me. When I went slumming like this, I wanted to cruise the bad slums. I wanted to hit Watts, the South Bronx, North Philly. From the cultural slumming point of view, Garth Brooks was little more than a slightly rundown neighborhood in Yonkers.

As the weeks passed, I grew fatigued with the numbing mediocrity of so many new experiences I had honestly hoped would be utterly appalling. The Radio City Easter Show was no lamer than any dozen of other spectacles I have seen on television over the years. I rented my first Steven Seagal movie (*Under Siege II*) and was dismayed to find that it was perfectly watchable. Neither "Jenny Jones" nor "Baywatch" was as rotten as I expected them to be, and *Reader's Digest* was merely boring, not unreadable. I'd been on the lookout for things that really stunk out the joint, yet somehow, I still felt that the Holy Grail of Horridness lay just outside my reach. What I really needed to find in order to purge myself forever of this unwholesome fascination with the cultural tar pits of America was to set out on a sacred quest, to travel to a shrine of suckiness, to bathe myself in the very Ganges of ghastliness.

It was time to make that pilgrimage to Atlantic City.

Entering Atlantic City by car is like entering Venice by dog cart—you simply must take the bus to get there. But when you get off the bus, after three hours of deadening chitchat with a battalion of cadaverous low rollers, you will immediately notice that Atlantic City does not resemble Venice. Atlantic City is a vast series of interlocking slums abutted by a narrow strip of clownish, high-rise buildings erected by people like Donald Trump. Venice is not. Even I, who have never been to Venice, know that.

Figuring that I should go first class all the way, I checked into the Taj Mahal, where my luggage was scooped up by a man dressed like Ali Baba. We deposited my bags, then I returned to the main floor, where I spent the next twenty-four hours gambling. I had never gambled before in my life, and did not know any of the rules. This was unfortunate because shortly after I arrived at the blackjack table, the young woman sitting directly to my left diplomatically informed me that I was "fucking the deck."

Fucking the deck, she explained, is the process whereby a neophyte or incompetent gambler disrupts the ordinary distribution of cards by making anomalous or stupid decisions. In my case, I stood on sixteen with the dealer showing a seven. According to orthodox blackjack procedure, you must always ask for another card when the dealer is showing a seven and you are holding sixteen, because you must always assume that the dealer has a concealed ten, ace, or face card.

But I had a funny feeling that my sixteen was good enough to win. Which it was. One by one, all the other players at the table went bust, as did the dealer. But now I was persona non grata, because I should have said "hit," and gone bust with the ten, whereupon the person sitting next to me would have gone bust with a nine, but the three other players farther down the table would have beaten the dealer. In short, it's not enough to win, you have to win according to the system. Thus, there was no joy in Mudville when the dealer paid me, because I had altered the platonic sequence of cards that the Lord intended, effectively *fucking the deck*.

I spent a good portion of the day fucking the deck at various tables, then around Happy Hour I ran into the young woman who had first pointed out my failings as a blackjack player. Over coffee, she explained the rules of blackjack. But she also explained the appeal of the game, pointing out that she didn't gamble because of the money, but because it was "Freudian."

"I like the table camaraderie," she noted. "You have to be careful not to disrupt the table camaraderie."

"How can you make sure that you don't disrupt the table camaraderie?" I inquired.

"Don't fuck the deck," she replied. "And if you do fuck the deck, try as hard as possible to unfuck it."

"How do you unfuck the deck?" I asked, not mentioning that I'd been accused of doing precisely that at least three other times during the day.

"It's a long story."

Up until this point, I was $120 ahead of the game by using my unconventional betting technique of standing when I felt like standing and hitting when I felt like hitting. But as soon as I started gambling the right way, I lost all my money. Before I knew it, I was $139 in the hole. For the life of me, I could not figure out what the attraction of this place was. The entire city was filled with doddering seniors, like the world's largest skittles league. Everyone had that bad South Philadelphia hair and that bad North Philadelphia attitude. The women in neo-Sumerian miniskirts who served you drinks all looked like Hittite linebackers. Everywhere you turned, a lounge lizardess who thought she was both Martha *and* the Vandellas was singing "Proud Mary," complete with Tina's extended verbal intro. Everybody at the blackjack table hated you because you'd fucked the deck. And you were down $139. At long last, I realized that I had come to the end of my journey. I had finally taken the ferry across the River Styx.

And wouldn't you know that when I disembarked from Charon's bleak craft, a Borscht Belt comedian would be waiting for me on the fatal shore? Yes, that very night, I was comped a ticket to a presentation of Freddy Roman's All-Star Revue, *Catskills on the Boardwalk*. As the show opened,

I was seated at a folding table parallel to the stage, right across from a man wearing a Medieval Tournament T-shirt and a Phillies cap, who seemed to be having some sort of an emotional meltdown. Glancing around, I noticed that I was forty-five years younger than anyone else in the room. And I was forty-five.

Finally, Freddy Roman, who is either a failed Henny Youngman or a successful Buddy Hackett, came out and told a joke about Bob Dole's hometown.

"In Russell, Kansas, it's so quiet, the town hooker is a virgin," he quipped.

The words weren't even out of his mouth before the crowd was in stitches.

Next, a Puerto Rican Wayne Newton sound-and-lookalike sallied forth to sing "Hello, Young Lovers" and "Unforgettable," backed by a band with more ponytails than the Cali cartel. Now, the crowd was wafted aloft on a rippling sea of ecstasy. If Perry Como himself had been there, they couldn't have been happier.

Next, a female comic dressed like George Burns wandered out and did a routine that included the line "When I was a young man, the Dead Sea was only sick."

The crowd got a lump in its throat just thinking about George.

Then a portly comic in a beret made a bunch of fart sounds.

The crowd completely lost it.

I hauled myself back to the $5 blackjack table, made a few bets, stood on the wrong card, fucked the deck. Most of the people at the table were quite civil, but a middle-aged man sitting in the last chair was livid.

"Must be using some new kind of counting system," he sneered, digging into his Croesian $45 stake and placing another bet. "Who needs this?"

That's when I realized it was time to go back to my old way of life. I'd been harangued for three hours on a bus by the Daughters of Rayon—a regiment of chronic losers who insisted that they always came out ahead when they visited Atlantic City. I'd been forced repeatedly to tip men dressed like Sinbad. I'd had to sit in stunned disbelief across from a yabbering buffoon while a female George Burns impersonator told jokes like "When I asked God what He thought of me in *Oh, God*, He said I was too young for the part." And now, for the fifth time in a single day I'd been accused of disrupting table camaraderie by fucking the deck. So there I sat at a $5 blackjack table in a glorified South Jersey slum, being dissed by a guy with a bad suit and a bad mustache and bad hair and a bad job and a bad family and a bad attitude, and it was all my fault that life hadn't turned out the way he planned. In short, I was getting the high hat from a low roller.

★   ★   ★

When I was coming of age in the late 1960s, most of my generation was involved in a heroic effort to depose Dean Martin, Desi Arnaz, Joey Bishop, and all the other cultural icons who ruled American society with an iron fist. This was an intellectual insurrection from which I defected by my twenty-first birthday. One reason I threw in the towel so quickly was because I knew that we couldn't win, that for every Rock Hudson we polished off, ten Rocky Balboas would spring up in his place. A month of Andrew Lloyd Webber musicals, Michael Bolton records, and Adam Sandler movies certainly helped jog my memory, but it was the two days in Atlantic City that confirmed what I'd suspected about America ever since I was a callow youth.

Somebody fucked the deck.

The Satanic Verses

When I returned from my trip to Atlantic City, I was convinced that I had seen the last of America's cultural cesspools. I had done my bit of slumming, dipped my toe in the River of Murk, and was now ready to return to my previous life as an effete, cynical snob.

But not long after I got back from the Taj Mahal, I realized that my curiosity about the Kingdom of Suck had not yet been sated. I had only gotten a glimpse at the horror, flitted around at the periphery of the abyss. I'd seen a few bad plays, read a few bad books, eaten a few bad meals. But I had at no point totally submerged myself in the quagmire. I was like Mosby's Rangers, making occasional forays into Yankee territory, then sneaking back to safety before darkness fell. I had never truly *invaded* my enemy's domain.

Months passed, but I could not remove that burr from my saddle. Finally, in October 1996, I decided to correct this situation, opting for a total immersion program, a cultural boot camp, as it were. I would spend the next year exhaustively exploring the world of bad books, bad food, bad movies, bad music, bad theater, bad travel, and bad ideas that made up what Tony Bennett once referred to as "The Good Life." Meanwhile, I would avoid—as far as was humanly possible— any of the intellectually uplifting experiences that had up until now brightened my existence.

Bad books seemed like a good place to begin.

It is no secret that the publishing world has been going downhill for some time. But critics have never been able to agree on precisely when the industry began to hit the skids. Personally, I think the decline can be traced to the year 1981, when the paperback edition of *Donahue: My Own Story* by Phil Donahue appeared. This book, whose hard-cover edition spent seven months on the *New York Times* best-seller list after it was published in 1979, is a classic example of the vanity of human wishes, illustrating that no matter how big a television star you are, and no matter how much interest the public once expressed in your childhood exploits with "Binky" Birt back in Cleveland and your youth-ful excitement at getting to interview Jumpin' Joe Kissinger, your autobiography is eventually going to wind up one of those sad, dog-eared, yellowing objects that peer up at emphysema-plagued old ladies from rummage sale booths.

I myself purchased a copy at a rummage sale, and as soon as I was done with it, it went straight into the fireplace. I know that people who remember the Nazi book-burnings say that it is a crime against humanity to burn books, but I don't think these people have read *Donahue: My Own Story*.

One reason the autobiographies of faded cultural icons deserve to end up in the incinerator is because all talk-show hosts write exactly the same memoir. The format runs some-thing like this:

1. Grew up on the tough streets of Philly, Cleveland, Omaha.
2. Had a big fight with someone named Binky or Legs.
3. Got to interview Jumpin' or Joltin' Joe something at first job at KRCA-Somewhere. Got goosebumps.
4. Married someone named Margie or Sue.
5. Got a big job in the big city.
6. Divorced Margie or Sue because we'd grown apart and someone named Marlo surfaced on the radar screen.
7. Became immortal.

This is not what depressed me about the book. The fact that a Phil Donahue could come and go without leaving much of a trace neither surprised nor distressed me; frankly, the vanity of human wishes is one of my favorite themes. When Shelley wrote that line in "Ozymandias"—"Look on my works, ye Mighty, and despair!"—he was referring specifically to books like *Donahue: My Own Story*. But, as I say, that's not what depressed me about the book. What depressed me was the fact that the paperback edition of the book had a forty-eight-page epilogue. That's right: forty-eight pages. Personal reflections. Book reviews. Correspondence. Even a cartoon by Garry Trudeau. Jesus wept. I like to think that forty-eight-page epilogues are reserved for people like Winston Churchill and Bertrand Russell, titans who put some real numbers up on the scoreboard, not some fatuous, blow-dried talk-show host from the Mistake by the Lake. But maybe that's just me.

After I read Donahue's autobiography, I couldn't help noticing how many other trashy writers appended epilogues and postscripts to their horrid *chefs d'oeuvre*. Having hacked my way through some of the least readable books ever written, I now found myself being forced to read about how the unreadable prose came to exist in the first place. This was the literary equivalent of being forced to watch a lengthy, painful bowel movement and then to be handed a detailed inventory of everything the creator had eaten in the previous twenty-four hours.

It amazed me how many of these gasbags adhered to this practice. The guns 'n' ammo guys often had an epilogue or postscript of some sort, where they thanked instructors from obscure military institutions who were even nuttier than they were. The horror novel loonies usually thanked some guy from Montana who had helped explain the concept of cybernecrocide to them. But even the romance novelists did it. Heather Graham, at the conclusion of her intensely silly Civil War bodice ripper *Rebel*, tacks on a nine-page chronology of the history of Florida. Question: How trustworthy is a nine-page chronology written by someone named Heather? And once the last petticoat has been torn free in the body of the novel, how many of her readers really care when Ponce de León reached the Florida Keys?

Another thing that annoyed me about our most popular writers was the tendency they had to include voluminous acknowledgments at the end of their books, as if anyone cared how Richard North Patterson came to write *The Final Judgment*. This is a long-winded murder mystery where unless you're a complete ninny you know who the murderer is by the end of the second chapter. Although the plot is filled with all sorts of twists and turns and red herrings, it's the usual generic crap about repressed New Englanders summering at Martha's Vineyard. It's just *so* obvious. Why then does Patterson feel it necessary to include this accolade at the end of the book:

"Most of all, there is my assistant, Alison Thomas. With each new day's writing, Alison helped me pick it apart—looking for weak spots; flaws in characterization; infelicitous language; and flagging plot lines. Writing is a solitary business; without Alison's keen eye and kind encouragement, it would be far more difficult. She has become a dear friend and an integral part of my work. For all those reasons, and more, this book is dedicated to her."

Oh, really? Well, sorry to break the news to you, Dick, but Alison's the one who left in the howler: "Blinded by seawater, Caroline felt the primal ocean envelop her." As for flagging plot lines, the whole book's a flagging plot line: Dad owned the knife; the knife is the murder weapon; Dad's probably the murderer. Nope, didn't take long to figure that one out.

Frankly, Mr. Patterson, I think Alison's starting to coast.

On several occasions, writers used a lengthy postscript at the end of the book to pay homage to themselves. After *Loves Music, Loves to Dance* finally reaches its conclusion, literary factory worker Mary Higgins Clark tacks on a fourteen-page self-interview in which she explains, among other things, how she came to write a novel about a serial killer who finds his victims through the personal ads in magazines.

Because everyone else had already written that book?

And at the end of *Journey*, megahack James A. Michener saw fit to include an epilogue entitled "Reflections," a masterpiece of self-delusion. After forcing his readers to slog through 278 pages of drivel about a quartet of late-nineteenth-century numbskulls who meet disaster in the Alaskan wilderness, Michener had to subject the audience to an additional twenty-eight long-winded pages explaining how he came to write this forlorn malarkey. The most outlandish moment, however, occurred when Michener, writing for a bunch of people who think the South Pacific Ocean is named after the musical, deconstructed the concept of "resonance."

Michener noted that this narrative technique had been used to great effect by artists as varied as Richard Wagner, Ludwig van Beethoven, Giuseppe Verdi, Leo Tolstoy, and Boris Pasternak. Explaining this concept to an audience that has to move its lips while reading his books is a little bit scary, like trying to explain cold fusion to a precocious hamster. And Michener's mentioning himself in the same breath as Balzac seemed a bit like Chris Darden mentioning himself in the same breath as Clarence Darrow.

The most obnoxious addendum I happened upon was the all-purpose letter that triumphant *New York Times* best-selling author LaVyrle Spencer writes to her readers at the end of *That Camden Summer,* a modern, village idiot's re-hash of *The Scarlet Letter.* The letter, written in that infuriating style of yuppie housewives who are too busy carpooling in the Range Rover to write individual messages to their dying grandmothers, reads like this:

Dear Reader,
It's been a busy year at the Spencer house, with so much activity that I wonder how I packed it all in and still got a book written.

She then goes on to explain how she miraculously found time to write her awful new novel about a country-and-western singer, which necessitated flying to Nashville to interview Reba McEntire, and then taking trips to Hawaii, New Zealand, Australia, Beijing, Hong Kong, India, Kenya, and England. (Note: Nashville is not usually included in this kind of itinerary.) There are plenty of details about the Sydney Opera House, the safari, the balloon trip. Then more information about her trips to Vancouver and Florida, some friends she met on the Concorde, and another trip to Hawaii, all of which must make her trailer-park readership feel pretty happy. Finally, she includes some photos of her grandchildren, of Reba McEntire, of some obviously bewildered Masai children at a game park in Kenya ("LaVyrle Spencer! I thought we were going to get to meet *Diana* Spencer!") and, of course, her "favorite guy," The Hubster.

As I fought my way through this material, I wondered why best-selling authors of the past hadn't thought to include such personalized addenda. Here's Anne Frank writing a letter to her readers at the end of her diary:

Dear Reader:
Oy! Yes, it's been a busy year at the Frank house, what with the Third Reich exterminating half the Jewish population of Holland, and I honestly don't know how I found time to write this book . . .

Or how about Peter Abelard?

Dear Reader:
Whew! That was some year chez les Abelards! Things started off well when I landed that big teaching job at the Sorbonne (finally got tenure). Also got quite a few manuscripts published in and around town. Then I met a fantastic girl named Eloise—loves music, loves to dance. Could be the one.

*On a down note, four ruffians did break into my Left
Bank apartment and cut my balls off back in Septem-
ber—don't know what that was all about! But hey, I'm
not the kind of guy to dwell on the negative.*
Best wishes in the New Year,
Love,
The Pete Man

Another trend I noticed while slowly working my way
through the Masters of Bilge canon was that bad writers like
to preface their books with a quote from somebody classy.
Thus, Mary Higgins Clark begins her serial-killer-by-
numbers novel *Loves Music, Loves to Dance* with a quote
from one of the biggest guns in all of Western civilization:

What is a friend?
A single soul dwelling in two bodies.

—ARISTOTLE

Not to be outdone, Nora Roberts kicks off her *Sweet
Revenge* with an excerpt from the Koran, Stephen Coonts
christens his *Flight of the Intruder* with a citation from
Ovid, and Stephen King ushers readers into *The Shining*
with quotes from both Francisco de Goya and Edgar Allan
Poe.

This made me wonder why great writers didn't start their
books with quotations from world-class hacks. Wouldn't it
be fun to open a reissue of *The Satanic Verses* by Salman
Rushdie and find this on the opening page:

"His eyes drank her in like wine, and she looked up at
him with a small smile."

—DANIELLE STEEL

Or this citation preceding the *Complete Tragedies of William Shakespeare*:

"The Hughes 500D is an extremely quiet helicopter due to sound baffles in the Allison 250-C20B engine."

—TOM CLANCY

Frequently, when reading the worst popular writers, I got the definite impression that they hadn't left the house in the past twenty years. Their estrangement from reality showed through most clearly not in their plots, which were uniformly absurd, but in their dialogue. You can see the point I'm driving at if you take a look at *Infamous* by Joan Collins or *Invasion* by Robin Cook. Collins is a thrillingly inept writer who in this case has crafted a semiautobiographical potboiler about a slutty TV star whose life is ruined by the media. Chockablock with ludicrous little Gallicisms ("Moi aussi," "voilà," "malheureusement," "cherie") that give Collins a chance to show off her sixth-grade French, the novel is not even vaguely readable. But what really sets her apart from routinely bad writers (say, her sister Jackie) is that Collins includes a couple of passages that underscore her complete self-exile from reality. For instance, the scene where the heroine's annoying teenage son gets in a bar fight with some peripatetic creep. What precipitates the fight is the thug's remark: *"Oh, yeah, who's gonna hurt me? You, you little punk? You couldn't hurt a pustule on a pimple."*

I've seen a few bar fights in my life, and I've witnessed quite a few altercations that could have turned into bar fights. But I've got to go on record here and say that in my experience, the phrase "You couldn't hurt the pustule on a pimple" is not the kind of remark you tend to hear in bars. Not in Los Angeles, where the novel is set. Not in New York. Not in North Philadelphia, where I grew up. And not in England, where Joan Collins grew up. Based on this Pustule on a Pimple interlude, I'd have to say that Joan Collins really needs to get out more.

Ditto Robin Cook. My favorite Cook book is *Invasion*, a clever thriller about extraterrestrials who contaminate human beings with a kind of mad cow disease that prompts them to gather in their pajamas in the middle of the night in suburban parking lots and decry the depletion of the ozone layer. In other words, transmogrifying an entire planet into a race of flannel-clad Al Gores. Reading the book, you get the impression that Cook is pretty solid on his prions and mad cow disease terminology, but doesn't have a clue how people speak in real life. This becomes readily apparent when one of the characters, Beau, gets into an altercation on a basketball court with a punk named Rocky. When Beau goes just a little bit too far with one of his condescending remarks, Rocky fires back: *"You're mighty arrogant for a little prig."*

I've been playing basketball for thirty-four years, and can state, without fear of being contradicted, that I have never heard anyone use the word *prig* on the court. "Cocksucker," yes. "Motherfucker," without question. "Faggot," more times than I can remember. But "prig"? Never. I think the term Robin Cook is looking for here is "prick." As in *cocksucking, motherfucking, faggot prick.*

Also, nobody named Beau plays basketball. Bo, yes. Beau, no.

★   ★   ★

And yet, even as I was tearing my hair out while consuming such arrant nonsense, I was developing an unhealthy affection for the Robin Cooks and the Joan Collinses of the world. Here's why. Earlier, I introduced the concept of *scheissenbedauern,* which is the feeling of regret one experiences when things you expect to suck do suck, but do not suck as much as you would secretly like them to suck. There is a related concept called *kleinebedauern.* This is the feeling of being emotionally shortchanged when something you expect to suck briefly attains the levels of suckiness that you desire, only to then retreat to a more ordinary level of suckiness. The problem with most bad writers is that they are mere sprinters. While LaVyrle Spencer and Joan Collins can sustain a high level of execrable writing for pages at a time, most of their contemporaries run out of gas after a few sentences.

For example, two-thirds of the way through her dull, predictable *Loves Music, Loves to Dance,* Mary Higgins Clark describes a woman who considers telling the police that her husband is a murderer but worries about the negative publicity.

"Donny. Beth. Trish. Conner. What would their lives be like if they grew up as the children of a serial killer?"

Well, Mary, they'd probably have a hard time getting baby-sitting assignments.

Sadly, Clark cannot sustain this level of ominous lunacy, quickly reverting to the isometrically ordinary prose style that is her stock-in-trade. Which, to return to my original point, is why I eventually came to develop a certain grudging admiration for Joan Collins. For one, she could invent terrific names like Jean-Jacques Costello. Two, her plots were as stupid as tomorrow's headlines. But more important, Collins knows that a bad book can't merely be intermittently bad; it has to be bad through and through. Here's how she describes Jean-Jacques's reaction to a technically inadequate blow job:

"Damn it, woman, you do that like you're milking a cow."

And her description of the heroine's trip to Venice: "The steep stone steps crumbled like Camembert as she scrambled up them."

What is so endearing about such industriously dim prose is not just its cryptic metaphors, not just its feud with logic, but its sheer volume. Lesser writers like Clark and Patricia Cornwell are only good for a few howlers per book. Joan Collins has them on every page. In this sense, the minor bad writers suffer from Vitas Gerulaitis syndrome: They can always pull off an occasional upset in the quarterfinals of Wimbledon, but when they get to Center Court for the grand finale, with the royal family watching and the eyes of the world trained on them, they choke.

Joan Collins doesn't choke. She sucks, but she doesn't choke.

As I delved deeper and deeper into the netherworld of popular culture, I came to depend more and more upon friends' recommendations. One friend told me that if I was looking for monstrously zany plots, I should check out V. C. Andrews. She was right on the money with that inspired suggestion. My first exposure to the author who has captivated more than 38 million readers with such titles as *If There Be Thorns* and *Petals on the Wind* was her remarkable *Flowers in the Attic*. According to the jacket copy, this was "the novel that began V. C. Andrews' extraordinary career."

What a book it was. A young widow, shut out of her dad's will because she married her uncle, who has now shuffled off this mortal coil, returns to her parents' home, determined to reclaim her inheritance. But her invalid father refuses to restore her name to his last will and testament unless she agrees to remain childless for the remainder of his life. This presents a bit of a problem since she already has four kids. Then a clever solution to her dilemma presents itself: She will lock the kids in the attic for many, many years until Pops finally kicks the bucket, by which time she'll be back in his good graces. Because the kids get food and a TV and are definitely not MIT material, they agree to go along with this game plan.

But then unexpected things start to happen. Mom's sadistic mother, who knows about the kids, forces her to strip naked and bullwhips her from head to toe. Then Granny jams a hypodermic into the young female narrator's arm and pours tar into her hair, forcing the kid to cut off her beautiful locks. Trapped in the attic for years, and now grown to young womanhood, the daughter finds it hard to get dates, so she reluctantly agrees to let her brother give her the old bone job. Now Grandma is really pissed, because the sins of the mother have been visited on the child, and the sins of the uncle have been visited on the niece/daughter/whatever, giving the novel a kind of biblical substructure. By this point, I was starting to suspect that most of V. C. Andrews's 38 million readers were inbreds who had bought her books at the Ozark branch of Barnes and Noble.

Meanwhile, Mom finds a dashing young lawyer to marry. As luck would have it, Poppy has now reinstated his daughter in his will, but still maintains the proviso that she loses her entire inheritance if she ever has any offspring. Weirder still, Mom has never bothered to tell her new husband that she has four kids. By this point, the kids realize that Mom has backed herself into a pretty tight corner. She doesn't want to lose all the money, and if she ever lets on to her husband that she has four kids locked away in the attic and is still subject to her mother's corporal punishment, he might think she's a little bit flaky. So it looks like the kids are locked up in the attic for the duration.

Eventually, one of the children dies. When Mom doesn't seem all that broken up about it, the kids start to figure out what the reader has pretty well sized up hundreds of pages earlier: Mom is a completely dysfunctional parent. Eventually, they accomplish the superhuman task of putting two and two together and realize that the sugar Granny has been lacing their breakfast cereal with over the years actually contains arsenic. So they finally decide to get the hell out of there, and hit the road. This is the way the saga ends.

There were a couple of things that I admired about this book. One, it started off at a high level of stupidity and kept getting stupider. For instance, the reason none of the maids or butlers around the house ever notice that there are four kids in the attic, despite what must have been Augean supplies of Cap'n Crunch and Lucky Charms disappearing from the larder, is that Grandma claims there are ferocious mice up there, and warns them to keep the door closed at all times. And everybody knows that mice couldn't possibly sneak down from the attic to the pantry unless the door was open.

The other thing I liked about the book was the fact that the novel that launched V. C. Andrews's extraordinary career did not appear to have been written by V. C. Andrews. On the copyright page of my dog-eared paperback, in tiny print, there is a little paragraph that reads:

Following the death of Virginia Andrews, the Andrews Family worked with a carefully selected writer to organize and complete Virginia Andrews' stories and to create additional novels, of which this is one, inspired by her story-telling genius.

In other words, if this announcement was correct, the novel that launched V. C. Andrews's extraordinary career was written after she was dead, as if *War and Peace* and *Anna Karenina* were written by one Chuck Prokoviev, a writer carefully chosen by the Count's devastated but cash-hungry survivors. Actually, it made perfect sense that V. C. Andrews's first book should have been written after she was dead because whoever wrote the book was obviously brain-dead. As was anyone who would pay good money to buy it.

Books did not have to be written by famous writers in order to be completely moronic. However, I did find that if I was in the market for a truly asinine book, the best way to find it was to visit my local bookstore and request any book sporting a blurb from Stephen King. It was through him I discovered not only the best-selling titans Clive Barker and Peter Straub but such less well known names as Bentley Little, Ronald Munson, Dan Simmons, and Stephen Dobyns. All were refreshingly stupid, especially Little ("A Master of the Macabre!"), whose novel *The Ignored* dealt with a crime wave perpetrated by people so bland that nobody even noticed when they showed up for work and jammed knives up their bosses' noses. Although I found each of these books bracingly vapid on its own merits, the critic in me noticed a pattern among writers that Stephen King held in awe. Almost without exception, the people he admired wrote big, thick, dumb, sadistic novels featuring emotionally arrested males and retarded plot lines in which:

1. Behind the seemingly innocent facade of a small town's rustic charm lurks *unspeakable horror, unspeakable evil*, or both;

2. Behind the door of the innocent little house at the end of the lane lurks *unspeakable horror*;

3. You can tell when the *unspeakable horror* that lurks down the seemingly innocent lane is about to switch into high gear because *that's when the author starts to use an awful lot of italics*;

4. The *unspeakable horror* frequently involves somebody getting his ear cut off.

Horror writers have been going after the eyes and the nose and the genitals for years, but what was most noticeable about the King-blurbed books that I read was the preponderance of auricular trauma. In Stephen Dobyns's *The Church of Dead Girls*, about which King had written, "If ever there was a tale for a moonless night, a high wind, and a creaking floor, this is it," the main suspect in a murder case bites off another guy's ear. King, incidentally, shares the same last name as Don King, the promoter of Mike Tyson's fights with Evander Holyfield, so I wouldn't be at all surprised if a fast check of Tyson's prefight reading material included Dobyns's book.

But it might also include fellow King blurbee Ronald Munson's *Night Vision*, a cyberthriller in which the bad guy cuts off a man's ear, and Dan ("I am in awe of Dan Simmons"—Stephen King) Simmons's *Children of the Night*, which positions Count Dracula or Vlad the Impaler or Whomever smack dab in the middle of the AIDS crisis, and which contains a lovely passage where short iron spikes are driven through a monk's ear.

Reading these books, I was struck by the intellectual poverty of the horror genre. Three years earlier I had written a story for *Movieline* magazine entitled "Lend Me Your Ears," explaining how ear mutilation was fast becoming the biggest cliché in the industry. In the first seventy-five years of its existence, the motion picture business lopped off just one ear of any consequence (in *Lust for Life*), but in the past decade ears had come off in movies as various as *Blue Velvet*, *Reservoir Dogs*, *The Last Temptation of Christ*, *Vincent and Theo*, and *Hard Target*, while ears were impaled in *Speed*, bitten in *Godfather III* and *A Perfect World*, and shot off in *Natural Born Killers*. In short, the whole ear thing was becoming a big joke.

Like all schlockmeisters, King blurbees had persuaded themselves that they were breaking new and daring ground, when in point of fact auricular butchery was fast becoming as hackneyed and old-hat as Doppler 4000 weather forecasts. But more significantly, they were borrowing techniques from bad movies in order to write bad novels that they hoped would be scary enough to get optioned by bad producers who would then hire bad directors to make them into bad movies where people get their ears cut off. *How postmodern.* To my way of thinking, they would have been far better off sticking with the old knife-through-the-eyeballs material that Clive Barker favored, both because it was more impressive on a purely visceral basis and because in some ways it seemed less clichéd.

I had another bone to pick with the horror genre. The back covers of horror novels always inform the reader that unspeakable horror lurks within. But in fact, the horror that lurks within is, invariably, eminently speakable. It's always a vampire or a ghost or a wraith or a satanic child or a dysfunctional Amish preteen or a hound from hell or a monster that looks like one of the creatures from *The Unnamable II* that's going to wrap its entrails around your throat, eat you, and then feed its feces—including you—to other hounds from hell. The horror that lurks behind the door or at the end of the lane or up in the attic or down in the basement is always a recognizably and even stereotypically horrific monster. We, as a people, have *been there, had our entrails ripped out by that.* It would really be a whole lot scarier for everyone involved if the winsome virgin who is the heroine of *The Church of Dead Dental Technicians* went up to the attic all alone on a dark and windy night without weapons or panties and with no neighbors within thirty miles and discovered that the unspeakable horror was actually Brent Musburger or one of those hostesses from the Home Shopping Network, the last people anyone would suspect of being hounds from hell. Then maybe the heroine could bite off *their* ears, just for a change.

That'd learn 'em.

The Howling

Books done, it was time to move on to films.

One day I spied an ad for a movie that promised to be deliciously horrible. *Gone Fishin'* starred Joe Pesci and Danny Glover as a pair of morons who go on a fishing trip in Florida and end up in a whole passel of trouble. The dead giveaway that the movie was going to bite—aside from the fact that both Joe Pesci and Danny Glover were in it—lay in the newspaper's blurbs:

> **"Holy Mackerel—You'll Laugh Your Bass Off!"**
> —*The Sandshark Sentinel*

> **"Thank cod for this movie!"**
> —*Saturday Evening Pike*

> **"Bring Your Whole Grouper to this movie!"**
> —*Barnacle and Seaweed Monthly*

In short, the movie was so bad that they couldn't even get Medved and that other pinhead to put in a nice word. Immediately, I decided it was a must-see. Late the next week, on the very last day the movie would be playing, I headed into town and turned up at the Sony Plaza complex at 68th and Broadway just in time for the 11:40 A.M. show. My intention at the time was to wait until the end of the film and then ask departing patrons how they had reached such an abject juncture in their lives where they had nothing better to do than to attend the 11:40 A.M. screening of a Joe Pesci movie. Co-starring Danny Glover.

But then I had a change of heart. When the film started rolling around 11:50, there were five of us in attendance, all men. About a third of the way through, one guy got up and left. Ten minutes later, another guy left. Then, about twenty minutes before the end of the film, a young computer sales-man–type way up in the front who had been the only person to laugh at anything said during the film also departed. That left me and a taciturn black senior citizen who did not seem to think the film was a laugh riot.

At the end of the film, the man got up from his seat and trudged out into the lobby. I followed him. I felt terribly sorry that a man who had lived through the Great Depression and had probably served in the Second World War and maybe even been wounded at Guadalcanal or Anzio should now, in the autumn of his years, find himself with nothing better to do than attend a Joe Pesci movie at eleven o'clock in the morning.

Then I got a wonderful idea.

"Excuse me, sir, may I talk to you for a second?" I asked.

"Yes?" he said, mildly suspicious.

"Sir, I represent the Joe Pesci Cultural Indemnification Institution and I have been personally authorized to refund your nine dollars for sitting through this horrible movie."

The man looked at me in disbelief as I handed him a five and four ones.

"Are you serious?"

"I am."

A radiant smile surged across his face.

"Man, that is just so *nice*."

It was, it really was. Although I had been contributing to philanthropic organizations like MADD and Greenpeace and the New York State Democratic Party for many years, I had never gotten any rush from my largesse. My donations had never given me any direct visceral jolt because I never got to see the whale, manatee, or doomed Guatemalan child that my largesse had rescued from perdition. But after I saw that wonderful smile spread across the old man's face, I decided that grassroots charity was the way to go. At long last, after all these years, I was going to be one, and perhaps even two, of the thousand points of light.

For the rest of the day, I positioned myself outside motion picture theaters when screenings of *Gone Fishin'* let out, and gave refunds to patrons who appeared to be suffering from extreme trauma. Sometimes I said I was from the Joe Pesci Cultural Indemnification Institute. Other times, I claimed I was a representative of the American Celluloid Retribution Society who had been authorized to give patrons complete refunds for sitting through very bad movies in the hope that word would spread throughout the community that not everyone in Hollywood was completely demonic. By the end of the day, I had given away ninety crisp one-dollar bills.

Two things stood out about the experience. One, a lot of the refundees were senior citizens, yet none of them volunteered the information that they had seen the movie at the seniors' rate, and had not paid the full $9 admission charge.

Second, a lot of the refundees didn't seem all that surprised to be getting the free moolah.

Typical was the exchange I had with a sixty-something woman, whom I immediately sized up as a native New Yorker.

"Ma'am, I represent an organization called the League of Cinematic Retribution, and I have been personally authorized to refund you the price of this appalling film."

"Thanks," she said, tucking the money away in her bag. "You do this a lot?"

"I do."

Her eyes lit up.

"Like where?"

"All over the place."

"Like what other films are you doing?"

I took my cue.

"Ma'am, wherever there's a movie starring Dan Aykroyd, look around; I'll be there. Wherever there's a movie starring Adam Sandler, Chris Farley, David Spade, or Pauly Shore, look around and I'll be there. Wherever people are being forced to watch movies starring Jennifer Aniston, David Schwimmer, Courteney Cox, or any of the members of the cast of "Friends," with the possible exception of *Scream,* where Cox has only a bit part and which was directed by cult favorite Wes Craven, I'll be there."

Again, she seemed nonplussed.

"Well, I'll be looking out for you."

I cannot adequately put into words the joyous feeling I came home with that day after restoring so many unsuspecting persons' faith in the American movie industry. I felt like Pope Leo I turning away Attila the Hun at the gates of Rome, like MacArthur returning to the Philippines, like Jesus giving Lazarus the kiss of life. Joe Pesci will do that to you. But as I lay down on my pillow that evening, I began to more closely examine my motives for this sudden munificence. And the more I thought about it, the more I realized that for as long as I could remember, I had always dreamed of the moment when a complete stranger would walk up to *me* and give *me* a complete refund for the movie I had just seen. In fact, I had always dreamed of the moment when a complete stranger would walk up to me and give me a complete refund for the last three hundred movies I had seen. Subconsciously, by compensating all these anonymous individuals for their suffering, I was trying to repay myself for the hours, days, and even years I had spent watching stupendously rotten motion pictures. At some deeply buried level of my consciousness, I was seeking vindication, compensation, and yes, perhaps even *closure*.

It was in this spirit that I now set out on a bold video-rental adventure. Here, my modus operandi was a bit different from what it would be with my other forays into the cultural Kalahari. Nothing in my work or personal life had ever required me to routinely read bad books, see bad plays, attend bad concerts, or eat in bad restaurants. If I wanted to eat, smell, hear, or read something atrocious, I had to make a conscious effort to do so. But because I had been a film critic for nine years, I had in the natural course of events seen most of the worst movies ever made. I had seen *Yentl*, *Shanghai Surprise*, *Yentl*, all the *Conan* films, *Yentl*. I had seen *Ishtar*, *Joe Versus the Volcano*, *Johnny Handsome*, *Who's That Girl?*, many, many unpleasant films starring Kiefer Sutherland, not to mention *Yentl*. I had seen all of Mickey Rourke's movies, and most of Mickey Rooney's. I had seen not one but two movies starring Paulina Porizkova. I had seen every movie about dentists ever made, including one in which Corbin Bernsen strangles his dental technician with a patient's pantyhose, then cuts his wife's tongue out. I had seen the entire oeuvre of the legendary Shannon Tweed. And, of course, I had seen *Yentl*.

Nevertheless, although I had watched literally thousands of bad films over the previous eight years, there were certain films that were so bad I had never dreamed of renting them. There was a reason for this. Very bad barbarian queen films starring Brigitte Nielsen and Grace Jones can always be placed in some kind of ironic context. They are beyond-belief awful, riveting in their unstinting dumbness. What's more, you usually get some pretty good shots of Sandahl Bergman in a paleolithically skimpy costume. While watching these movies, you get a definite sense that you are watching what will be viewed as the Godzilla movies of tomorrow: films that future generations of twenty-somethings will deem cult classics, debating long into the night whether Brigitte Nielsen's best work was done before or after she met Mark Gastineau. Future generations of young people will do this not out of any real affection for Ms. Nielsen or Ms. Bergman, but because they know that it will annoy their parents, who will forever be admonishing that they really ought to be watching the Turner New Classics like *The Piano* and *The Shawshank Redemption*.

But to my way of thinking, there was no ironic context in which I could place Burt Reynolds movies. There was no way that Jackie Gleason's performances in the *Smokey and the Bandit* movies could be rehabilitated through the sacred balm of camp. There was no way that *Porky's* or *Police Academy* could be transmuted into cult classics like *The Three Amigos* or *Can't Stop the Music*. These were movies that just plain sucked. They sucked when they were being pitched, they sucked when they were being made, they would suck for all eternity. William Goldman, the famous screenwriter of *Butch Cassidy and the Sundance Kid* and many other fine films, once said that almost all films originally started out with the intention of being good, but then were sabotaged, plagued by cost overruns, or simply lost their way.

The movies I was planning to rent didn't fall into that category. They were primally unwatchable. And now it was time to watch them. Yes, if I was really serious about plumbing the depths of popular culture, it was time to hit the video store and systematically rent every movie I had consciously refused to suffer through during my trying decade as a movie critic. It was time to watch every movie I had never watched in my entire life simply because no complete stranger had ever walked up to me and given me $9 as an incentive.

Hollywood is never more awe-inspiring than when it gets things completely wrong. Think of Bill Murray as a globe-trotting intellectual in *The Razor's Edge*. Think of Robert Mitchum as a pussy-whipped cuckold in *Ryan's Daughter*. Think of Sharon Stone as a pistol-packing momma in *The Quick and the Dead*. Think of Demi Moore as anything in anything. But mostly think of Bill Murray in *The Razor's Edge*. No, mostly think of Demi Moore as anything in anything. Casting Moore as a woman who has come to the New World so that she can "worship without fear or persecution" in *The Scarlet Letter* is like casting Bruce Willis as Young René Descartes.

Of course, *Striptease* was even better. This is the film where Demi Moore, locked in an ugly custody battle, loses her job working for the FBI and has to get a job as a stripper, thus permanently putting to rest the theory that government bureaucrats cannot find gainful employment in the private sector. Worthwhile if only to see Burt Reynolds dressed in cowboy boots, boxer shorts, a leather vest, and a cowboy hat while completely covered in Vaseline, the film is worthwhile if only to see Burt Reynolds dressed in cowboy boots, boxer shorts, a leather vest and a cowboy hat while completely covered in Vaseline.

But sporting the yarmulke was also a nice touch.

One thing that I admire about films like *Striptease* is that they serve as powerful reminders that on any given day Hollywood has the potential to release the worst film in history. Purists like to think that no one will ever make a worse movie than Ed Wood's *Plan 9 from Outer Space* or *Invasion of the Killer Tomatoes*. Bullshit. Purists are like those crotchety old-timers who insist that there will never be a worse team than the 1972–73 Sixers. Then along come the 1997–98 Nuggets to blow the Sixers right out of the water.

Bad-movie buffs' knee-jerk veneration of the good old bad days is nonsense: Hollywood studios released *Striptease* and *Showgirls* within weeks of each other, and quickly followed up with *The Scarlet Letter,* proving that, when they set their mind to it, they can make bad movies by the fistful. And that's just the big-ticket bad movies. Don't forget the indies. One day I went to see *Good Luck,* a film starring Gregory Hines as a paraplegic dental technician who persuades Vincent D'Onofrio, a blind football player, to enter a white water–rafting contest with him. It was the only time in my life that I sat and watched a movie without one other person being in the theater. In fact, the theater was so eerily quiet that afternoon that I'm not even sure I was there.

The purists' idea of a bad film is one that is deliberately bad or so cheap that it could never be any good. That's not my idea of a bad film. The way I see it, most truly bad motion pictures cost a fair amount of money to make, and are conceived with major pretensions to excellence, only to end in abject humiliation for everyone involved. They are mistakes—big mistakes. For a movie to ascend to the Parnassus of Putrescence, there usually has to be a sense that the film is in some way either a financial, artistic, or moral catastrophe, not an inadvertent monstrosity like a Mexican hairless or Dennis Rodman. Think *Cleopatra*. Think *At Long Last Love*. Think *Heaven's Gate*. Think of movies that not only wreck careers, that not only wreck studios, but that wreck entire decades.

But there is another kind of bad movie worthy of our attention: The ensemble bad flick. It was to this category that I next turned, and where better to start than with the master? Mel Brooks's *History of the World, Part I* and *Robin Hood: Men in Tights* are sublime examples, but an even more satisfying experience lay in store for me in Brooks's *Spaceballs*, a crude parody of *Star Wars*, which not only stars Rick Moranis, Daphne Zuniga, Bill Pullman, Joan Rivers, Dick Van Patten, John Candy, and many other repeat offenders, but which includes such lines as: "What's the matter, Colonel Sanders? Chicken?"

Obviously, these three movies were atrocious. But they were atrocious in a respectable, highly professional way, like an Elton John concert. They were brutally unwatchable movies made by someone who knew how to make a brutally unwatchable movie, not somebody who had just lucked out. This trio of rewardingly fulsome viewing experiences prompted me to reflect on the lost art of the truly bad movie.

In recent years, owing to the cultural suzerainty of "Saturday Night Live," bad comedies had succumbed to a very unsatisfactory formula. A simpleton named Sandler, Farley, Aykroyd, Belushi, Piscopo, etc., was cast as the main character in an inane film and surrounded by an ensemble of talentless, generally obscure supporting players. This was the template for movies as varied as *Happy Gilmore*, *Airheads*, *Beverly Hills Ninja*, *Black Sheep*, *Tommy Boy*, and *The Great Outdoors*. Because the centrifugal force driving the film was the bad star or bad co-star, the films early on attained their maximum level of idiocy and pretty much stayed there. The films could not get much worse, because the stars themselves were incapable of getting any worse. They had *minned* out.

In some cases, the directors of these films capriciously diluted the toxic potencies of these appalling motion pictures by failing to edit out an unexpectedly competent performance (Joe Mantegna in *Airheads*), or an amusing cameo (Kevin Nealon in *Happy Gilmore*). This was a huge mistake, for to the connoisseur of the bad film, there is nothing worse than a bad film ruined by a few good jokes, an intelligent observation, or a jarringly professional performance. It also raises the larger philosophical question of what kind of society rewards cretins like Adam Sandler and Chris Farley, but forces decent, intelligent human beings like Kevin Nealon to play bit parts in their movies. But that is a subject for another day.

In sharp contrast, Mel Brooks came from the old school of bad films. Brooks understood that for a bad film to truly succeed, it must start out at a vertiginously high level of badness and then somehow, miraculously, get worse. The secret to this lay not in the material but in the casting. The one foolproof mechanism that can be used to ensure that a bad film keeps getting worse is to keep introducing more and more washed-up old coots in unexpected cameo appearances. Brooks realizes that if you start with Sid Caesar, you have to finish with Henny Youngman, that if you set the trap with Dick Van Patten, you must spring the trap with Richard Lewis. Brooks understands that for a truly bad movie to succeed, the audience must be reduced to a perpetual state of dread, wondering if and when Don Knotts is going to turn up. For if Don Knotts is already here, Tim Conway cannot be far away.

But Brooks does not stand alone in the enchanted circle of bad movie makers. Hal Needham is also a force to be reckoned with. One day I stopped by my local video store to pick up a copy of his 1981 film *The Cannonball Run. The Cannonball Run* was one of those films that I had long viewed as the cinematic equivalent of a bone-marrow transplant: If things had gotten this bad, I might just as well die. As luck would have it, the day I stopped by Videophile, the proprietress told me that her copy of *Cannonball Run* had vanished from the shelves. But she did have Needham's *Cannonball II* in stock. Was I interested?

I was, I was. Several years earlier, I had written a story for *Movieline* in which I looked at more than twenty Part III's from series where I had never seen Parts I and II, just to see if the sequel to the sequel made any sense. Most of them were unbearable, but *Child's Play III* was so good that I went back and looked at the original, which was just fantastic. More recently, I had spent an entire week looking at sequels to movies I had never seen. Again, the results had been tremendously satisfying. *976-EVIL 2*, a film I would have rented for the title alone, seemed to apotheosize the genius of Hollywood with its seductive premise: A bunch of randomly selected but thoroughly ordinary people happen upon mysterious business cards inviting them to call a number for their "Horrorscope." Once they dial the number, the phone imbues them with extraordinary supernatural powers that enable them to solve their problems. But gradually the phone takes over their lives and unleashes pure evil on everyone who comes anywhere near them.

I was sure Geraldo Rivera had one of these cards in his wallet.

That film was a perfect example of something I expected to be awful that unexpectedly turned out to be far worse than I could have ever envisioned in my wildest dreams. But no Part II that I had seen could match *Cannonball Run II* for the depth and sweep of its awfulness. Just consider the list of players as it appears at the beginning of the film:

Burt Reynolds
Dom DeLuise
Dean Martin
Sammy Davis, Jr.
Jamie Farr
Marilu Henner
Telly Savalas
Shirley MacLaine

Pretty scary, *n'est-ce pas?* Especially considering that the cast also included Ricardo Montalban, Don Knotts, and Doug McClure. Needless to say, the film got off to a roaring start and never took its foot off the pedal. First, Dom De-Luise did a wonderful parody of Marlon Brando's Godfather. Then Susan Anton bent over to show off her incredibly tight pants. Then Charles Nelson Reilly played the Don's son, Don. That is, Don Don. Then Catherine Bach bent over to show off her incredibly tight pants. Then Sammy Davis, Jr., cast as a Catholic priest sporting a cowboy hat, showed up, with Dino, also disguised as a priest, right alongside. This was a scene that seemed to illustrate, once again, how terribly far the Catholic Church had strayed from the straight and narrow path back in the 1970s in its desperate attempt to seem "with it."

What I most admired about *Cannonball Run II* was the way its studiously substandard cast of performers kept getting relief from even worse reinforcements. It was as if the federal government, fearing an alien invasion, had financed a movie that could be shipped into Outer Space as proof that no intelligent life form could survive on this planet. But more to the point, everyone involved in the making of this film seemed to recognize that a bad movie is like a shark: Unless it keeps moving, it will die.

Today's bad filmmakers don't know how to make a bad movie on the scale of a *Cannonball Run II*. They cheat. They skimp. They cut corners. Back in the good old days, the powers-that-be knew that Burt Reynolds, Dom DeLuise, and Charles Nelson Reilly didn't pack enough firepower to get the job done. It wasn't enough to have Sammy as a bogus priest and Shirley MacLaine as a whore masquerading as a nun. It wasn't enough to have Ricardo Montalban kiss an orangutan and tell Jamie Farr: "Now, if your mother could kiss like that!" It wasn't enough to have a guest appearance by Old Blue Eyes himself. No, to make things really work, you still needed Jackie Chan beating the shit out of a bunch of bikers. You still needed guest appearances by Tony Danza and Mel Tillis. You still needed cameos by Jim Nabors and the moron who used to play Goober on "Mayberry, R.F.D." Finally, you still needed Don Knotts and Tim Conway serenading a chimpanzee with a stirring rendition of "By the Light of the Silvery Moon."

I came away from this movie awed by the sheer professionalism of everyone involved. To me it was now clear that people like Lorne Michaels and Adam Sandler and Chris Farley and Steve Guttenberg were merely blips on the cultural radar screen. They were like the Bud Grant Minnesota Vikings, perennial contenders who just couldn't seem to win the big one. The folks who made *Cannonball Run II* were like the '27 Yanks of bad movies. And believe you me, before this journey had run its course, I was definitely going to be renting the original *Cannonball Run*. If it was the last thing I ever did.

Sadly, the capacious joys of *Cannonball Run II* made it impossible for me to enjoy bad films of slightly lesser pedigree. Once again, I was afflicted with *scheissenbedauern*. *Police Academy*, a film about a cabal of dingdongs who become police officers, was absolutely putrid, but without a guest appearance by Hervé Villechaize or Jim Nabors, it left me kind of cold. I felt exactly the same way about *Porky's*, a Gulf Coast *American Graffiti* in which a bunch of Eisenhower-era redneck morons dream of screwing cheerleaders. The most profitable film to ever come out of Canada, the film also starred Alex Karras, who used to be Howard Cosell's partner on "Monday Night Football." With all these elements in place, it should have been much, much worse than it was. But it wasn't.

It was time to turn things up a notch or two.

When the opening credits for *St. Elmo's Fire* start to roll, these are the names you see, arranged in neat, alphabetical order:

Emilio Estevez
Rob Lowe

Andrew McCarthy
Demi Moore
Judd Nelson
Ally Sheedy
Mare Winningham

As my eyes wandered over the cast of characters, I tried hard to remember when I'd last seen a list of names that scary. The 1962 New York Mets? That famous Ted Danson roast at the Friar's Club? Then it came to me: The Nuremberg Rally of 1934, where the list read:

Joseph Goebbels
Herman Göring
Rudolf Hess
Heinrich Himmler
Adolf Hitler

And believe you me, do you ever get your money's worth! Scum-sucking yuppie pigs cheat on each other, snort coke, play sax, get laid. Yes, *St. Elmo's Fire* is one of those touchstone films, like *Cocktail* and *Bright Lights, Big City*, that remind us that the eighties were far, far worse than any of us can recall today, and that by helping these monsters get their careers off the ground, we will all be paying for our sins for decades to come.

From *St. Elmo's Fire,* it was a natural leap to another mid-eighties war crime, *The Breakfast Club*. This is the movie where Judd Nelson, Molly Ringwald, Ally Sheedy, Anthony Michael Hall, and Emilio Estevez play monstrous teen scum trapped in a detention room for an entire day, and you are trapped there with them. Yet, having watched *The Breakfast Club* in its entirety, I had to own up to a grudging respect for the innovative bad work of John Hughes. Unlike Mel Brooks and the producers of *Cannonball Run II,* who loaded up their movies with tired old farts, Hughes reversed that equation by using a battalion of tired young farts who would one day become the Ricardo Montalbans of their generation. Thus, Hughes had created an entirely new genre: Preemptive Burnout Cinema. Here, in a nutshell, is the formula for the classic John Hughes bad movie:

1. The movie must launch the careers of actors who will ruin American civilization for decades to come.
2. The movie must deal with bogus class warfare.
3. The movie must start out at a high level of awfulness and progressively get worse, if necessary by giving Ally Sheedy more lines.

Two other films from this period worthy of note are *Sixteen Candles* and *Pretty in Pink,* both of which represent pivotal moments in the history of the Republic. There are certain crossroads in American history at which this otherwise wonderful society takes a wrong turn, then continues down this errant path for a very long time. Such a moment occurred in the 1960s with Julie Andrews, in the late 1970s with John Denver, and in the mid-1980s with Molly Ringwald. And yet one of this country's problems is that it has a hard time admitting that it has made a mistake. Americans don't want to be reminded that they elected Richard Nixon by a colossal margin in 1972. They don't want to be reminded that they voted for Jimmy Carter. And they certainly don't want to be reminded that they bought all those Peter Frampton records.

Personally, I do not believe that America can ever become a truly healthy society until it publicly apologizes to the rest of the world for the pain it has caused. Just as the Germans had to apologize for mustard gas, Auschwitz, and Horst Buchholz, the American people must one day apologize to the rest of the world for Jim Croce and Molly Ringwald. For this great nation to be fully cleansed of the blight on our history caused by *The Breakfast Club* and *Sixteen Candles*, the person who made the decision to put Molly Ringwald on the cover of *Time* magazine in the mid-eighties must step forward, don sackcloth and ashes, and agree to ritual flaying and disembowelment. It's the only way we can emerge in the bold light of history and assume the mantle of greatness for which we have long been destined.

Little by little, my fascination with the cinematically retrograde was growing to the point where I was faced with an insatiable need to kick things up into a higher gear. Increasingly, I found myself engaging in weird rituals, such as beginning a sequel marathon with *Nightmare on Elm Street V*, then working my way through parts IV, III, II, I. This was not wholesome. Another day I made a list of terrifying, but completely unrelated, horror sequels and started watching them in rising numerical order just to see what kind of rush I would get.

First came *The Unnamable II*. This is a movie that asks the question: Can two creatures occupy the same space in the universe when one is human and the other is a monster? Of course, they can: Just watch "Regis & Kathie Lee." I next checked out *Children of the Corn III*, an ingenious film that deals with a sinister Amish child plagued by an unhealthy interest in maize products of vaguely supernatural provenance. Eventually, he moves to Chicago and gets himself adopted by a commodities trader. Not surprisingly, the child turns out to be Satan. Not surprisingly, so does the commodities trader.

Next stop was *Body Chemistry IV*. It is always a bad sign if the opening credits to a movie contain the words: "And Chick Vennera as Freddie Summers." This is just one of those little things that, as a movie critic, you pick up over the years. Needless to say, the movie was very bad. But not as bad as *Halloween V*, where even Jason seems to be tired of being Jason. From *Halloween V*, I effortlessly segued into *Howling VI: The Freaks*.

One of the things I like about watching cheaply made sequels is that you often cross paths with old friends. And I'm not just talking about people like Shannon Tweed, who spend their entire careers making sequels. No, what I find interesting is when you're watching a film like *The Unnamable II* and an old trouper like Peter Breck ("The Big Valley") pops up. It's almost like visiting a bar in Acapulco and discovering that your old high school phys. ed. teacher is the bathroom attendant.

A perfect example was *Howling VI*, where the very first credit to appear was the name "Carol Lynley." My heavens, what had Carol Lynley done that she should merit this kind of celluloid banishment? And what was this type of film a stepping stone to? And why did she make her exit from the movie so soon? Anyway, it was nice to see she was still working, if only because it raised the possibility that Pamela Sue Martin might turn up in *Howling XII*. Hopefully still sporting those hot pants she wore with such consummate aplomb in *The Poseidon Adventure*.

From *Howling VI*, I moved on to *Witchcraft VII*, a generic vampire movie with little to recommend it. By this point it was about ten o'clock at night and I really wanted to end the day of uninterrupted horror with a big bang. Meticulously, I recapped my viewing diet for the day. Since I'd switched on the VCR and television at nine in the morning, I had seen an impressive array of werewolves, vampires, demons, hyperthyroid annelids, and, of course, wraiths. I had witnessed innumerable beheadings, garrotings, disembowelings. I had watched people get their eyes torn out, their limbs chopped off, their heads sliced off with scythes. I had seen demonic cornstalks draw and quarter a farmer, and had looked on in disbelief as a fiend drove a spike through the back of a woman's head. But nothing that I had subjected myself to in the course of the day in any way prepared me for my final selection, the most stomach-turning spectacle of all.

Ali MacGraw and Ryan O'Neal in *Love Story*.

I had long avoided the megahit of 1970 because I suspected that Jimi Hendrix's death may have had something to do with watching this film on a full stomach. Luckily, I hadn't eaten all day, because there was one scene that definitely would have brought it all up. That's the sequence where the *über*preppy scion O'Neal is disowned by his father, then goes to visit the dean of his prospective law school and asks for a scholarship, claiming to be "destitute." When the dean points out that scholarships are generally reserved for people who do not have any money, O'Neal retorts: "Why should I be penalized because I was once related to a rich man?" It is clear from the way the scene is played that the filmmaker is definitely in O'Neal's corner.

Pass me the airsickness bag.

What I hadn't realized about *Love Story* in the quarter-century I had given it such a wide berth was that it was responsible for introducing most of the dominant themes that would ravage America throughout the eighties and nineties: lawyers, lawyers who play racquetball, lawyers who play racquetball who marry women named Jennifer, lawyers who play racquetball who marry women named Jennifer who like to masquerade as poor people, and, of course, ice skating. The fact that the film enjoyed such popularity, and relatively recent popularity, is a cause for grave concern. As I pointed out earlier, movies such as this form a major part of our cultural heritage; they are not harmless bagatelles that we can simply shrug off. Just as Germany is still infested by people who fought enthusiastically for the Third Reich, American society is still inhabited by people who saw this movie, or worse still, made this movie. They walk among us. They bide their time. They await their moment. One day, not unlike the South, they will rise again.

For the rest of us, this is no time to let down our guard. Remember: Eternal vigilance is the price of eternal freedom. Evil triumphs not when bad men do bad things but when enough good men stand by and do nothing. And those who cannot remember the past are condemned to repeat it, often by watching overpriced Ali MacGraw exercise videos.

A final word. Like most of Oliver Stone's movies, *Love Story* is a film that labors under the mistaken assumption that the main characters are saintly. But like Jim Garrison in *JFK* and Jim Morrison in *The Doors,* the characters played by Ryan O'Neal and Ali MacGraw in *Love Story* are odious hydras who deserve to have all their heads chopped off. Ray Milland, the tight-assed son of a bitch who tosses his son out into the street, is the only likable character in the entire movie.

Indeed, as the film raced toward its mawkish conclusion, I was kind of hoping that Pops would recommend a back-alley oncologist who would deliberately bungle MacGraw's treatment just to make sure she was dead. Not since Alan Ladd gunned down Jack Palance at the end of *Shane* was I so happy to see someone bite the dust. Remember, shortly before MacGraw finally kicks the bucket, she says to O'Neal: "I went to Radcliffe . . . I once knew all of the Mozart Köchel listings." Then she adds: "What number is the A-Major Concerto?"

Die, witch, die.

Only the Good Die Young

One day I noticed that I was getting a bit puffy, so I decided that I should start going to the gym. Here I discovered a strange phenomenon that may explain why so many people in my general age group have trouble losing weight. The first time I trudged into the YMCA exercise room around the corner from my office, the Classic Rock radio station blaring through the loudspeakers was playing Phil Collins's "In the Air Tonight." The second time I went, the radio was playing The Eagles' "Witchy Woman," but two songs later, it segued into Phil Collins's cover of the Supremes' "You Can't Hurry Love." And the third time I dragged myself over there, the radio was playing Collins's "I Missed Again."

It was now apparent to me that if I was going to lose any weight, I was going to have to listen to an awful lot of Phil Collins records in the process. But how many? The very next day, I bought a notebook and reported to the gym. Deciding that I needed to lose 15 pounds in 15 weeks, I figured that I could accomplish this by burning off 500 calories a day, which would work out to 3,500 calories (or one pound) a week. So I spent half the time on the Stairmaster and half the time on the exercise bicycle, reading newspapers.

Every time a new song came on the radio, I would mark it down in my notebook. I did this for one entire week, and the results were terrifying. The first day I worked out in the gym, I heard Rod Stewart's "Reason to Believe," Golden Earring's "Radar Love," Billy Joel's "The Stranger," Survivor's "Eye of the Tiger," Elton John's "Levon," Chicago's "Saturday in the Park," Kim Carnes's "Bette Davis Eyes," and Phil Collins's "Sussudio." I burned off five hundred calories.

The next day, I heard Rod Stewart's "Stay with Me," Elton John's "Bennie and the Jets," The Eagles' "Witchy Woman," Meat Loaf's "Paradise by the Dashboard Light," Eddie Money's "Baby, Hold On," Kenny Loggins's "Footloose," Billy Joel's "We Didn't Start the Fire," and Phil Collins's "I Missed Again." I burned off four hundred calories.

On my next trip to the gym, I heard Billy Joel's "It's Still Rock 'n' Roll to Me," The Eagles' "Witchy Woman," Elton John's "Goodbye, Yellow Brick Road," Eric Clapton's "Tears in Heaven," and Phil Collins's "In the Air Tonight." I burned off three hundred calories.

Eventually, after about nine more trips to the gym over a three-week period, I was able to burn off one full pound. But it was now clear that unless I was prepared to change gyms, I would have to continue this Witchy Woman Diet and hear "Peaceful, Easy Feeling" and "Sussudio" at least five times for every pound that I lost. Since I was interested in shedding fifteen pounds, this worked out to seventy-five listenings of each song. Initially, I thought I might be equal to the task, but what I discovered in the course of my research is that each pound becomes progressively more difficult to shed, because the Eagles and Phil Collins have a kind of cumulative, deleterious effect on the nervous system. It is not true that what doesn't kill you makes you stronger. What doesn't kill you now will simply kill you later.

And it wasn't just a question of Phil Collins and the Eagles. By the time I had lost my second pound, I had also listened to Billy Joel's "She's Always a Woman" four times and Bob Seger's "Against the Wind" thrice. I don't need to tell you how the story ends: I never lost the fifteen pounds.

Round about this time, a senseless tragedy with classic rock–format overtones occurred in midtown Manhattan. In February 1997, a Middle Eastern maniac shot a bunch of people on the observatory deck of the Empire State Building, killing a young Danish musician. A couple of days later, I read in the newspaper that Dave Herman, the legendary morning deejay for New York's now-fallen-on-hard-times WNEW radio station, would be broadcasting his entire show from high atop the skyscraper. The deejay would also be giving away memorabilia associated with the famous building in an effort to dispel the gloom.

The morning of the broadcast, I tuned into the show and listened as Herman played an assortment of upbeat songs in an effort to put "a positive spin" on both the building and the city. Ironically, one of the songs was by the Grateful Dead. Inevitably, one of the songs was Billy Joel's "New York State of Mind." Which immediately raised the question: Is a Middle Eastern terrorist who goes all the way to the top of the Empire State Building to gun down seven innocent people really all that much worse a human being than a deejay who goes all the way to the top of the Empire State Building to play Billy Joel songs?

That afternoon, I went out and bought the entire Billy Joel catalog, deciding that it was time I gave his work a closer listen. I have always had a grudging admiration for Joel, because his first major album, *Piano Man*, is a frank, no-holds-barred, cultural early-warning system of the horrors that lay ahead. On an album that contained just nine tracks, the precocious Joel had managed to write four songs that even now, two decades later, still stand alone as masterpieces of lameness. *Piano Man* opens with the festively corny "Travelin' Prayer," a banjo-laden number best thought of as Great Neck bluegrass, followed by the criminal "Piano Man," the putrid "The Ballad of Billy the Kid," and the nauseating "Captain Jack." To my knowledge, no other artist in the history of popular music has ever been this bad this early in his career. And no artist has ever remained as consistently bad for such a long time. No other artist has written so many songs that on first hearing immediately qualified for that Desert Island Dream List you'd compile for your worst enemy.

It was not always clear that this was going to be the case. *Street Life Serenade,* the album that followed *Piano Man,* was a bit of a disappointment, since the only truly memorable bad songs were "Los Angelenos" and "The Entertainer." However, with *The Stranger,* Joel truly hit his stride. By recording "Just the Way You Are," "Movin' Out," "Only the Good Die Young," "Get It Right the First Time," "The Stranger," "She's Always a Woman," and "Scenes from an Italian Restaurant," Joel had come close to making the perfect bad album. Indeed, had Joel merely left off the humdrum "Vienna" and "Everybody Has a Dream," which ends the record, it would have been an LP consisting of nothing but archetypally horrible songs. It would have been the worst album ever made. In fact, I think it *is* the worst album ever made. But I still think it could have been worse.

Though many artists would have been daunted by the task of topping an album as unremittingly awful as *The*

Stranger, Joel continued to show his mettle by releasing the exquisitely rotten *52nd Street* and the unlistenable *Turnstiles*. However, after this opulently foul LP, Joel started to show signs of flagging. While *Glass Houses* (1980) included "Don't Ask Me Why" and "It's Still Rock 'n' Roll to Me," it was now obvious that as Joel's career proceeded, the ratio of abysmal songs to merely bad ones slowly declined. Songs like "Sleeping with the Television On" were nondescript, not the defiantly rotten material of his early records. Similarly, while *The Nylon Curtain* (1982) got off to a good start with "Allentown," "Pressure," and "Goodnight Saigon," the remainder of the album was mostly filler.

In no way, shape, or form am I suggesting that *An Innocent Man* is anything less than a bad album. However, the very fact that it was a doo-wop album imposed finite limits on its awfulness. Doo-wop, in and of itself, is already the worst music in American history, the kind of background music one associates with bars where people like Danny Aiello hang out. As such, the record is essentially a parody of a self-parodying art form by a man who never really had his heart in rock 'n' roll in the first place. I found the whole thing terribly confusing.

Joel's dismal but uneven recording career continued with generic records like *The Bridge*, *Storm Front*, and *River of Dreams*. Throughout, there were flashes of the old genius, for Joel never lost the endearing ability to make a complete fool of himself. While his later albums contain nothing as pathetic as "Captain Jack" or "Always a Woman to Me," there are occasional pearls of boisterous foolishness: his absurd fisherman song, and the ridiculous Russophilic "Leningrad." Like an aging gunfighter, he can no longer suck as bad and he can no longer suck as often. But catch him on the wrong day when the sun is high behind him and he'll put a bullet right between your eyes.

The big question today is whether Billy Joel has one truly bad record left in him. Frankly, I do not know the answer to this question. Perhaps we should just be grateful for what we have. Joel at least has hung around; Karen Carpenter upped and died, spoiling everything. One way to put all this in perspective is to compare his career to that of Phil Collins. A couple of years ago, Jimmy Guterman and Owen O'Donnell wrote a book called *The Worst Rock 'n' Roll Records of All Time* in which they ranked Joel as the worst rocker ever, with Collins holding down the No. 2 spot. This is an assessment with which I would wholeheartedly agree.

However, I would hasten to point out that the gap between No. 1 and No. 2 is oceanic. In the sport of baseball, Babe Ruth may well be the greatest ballplayer of all time, but he gets serious competition from Ty Cobb, Willie Mays, Ted Williams, Hank Aaron, and several others. Many, perhaps most, classical music aficionados would put Mozart at the top of the heap of composers, but the fact that others would give Bach or Beethoven the nod for the No. 1 spot indicates that Mozart's edge is by no means gargantuan. Michael Jordan may be better than Wilt Chamberlain, but not by much.

In the case of Phil Collins and Billy Joel, the issue is far more clear-cut. Collins has written many, many bad songs. But they tend to be bland and overproduced rather than catchy. Phil Collins has one annoying trick that he uses over and over again: those irksome Miami Sound Machine horns wailing away in the background, creating a pseudo-Carnival atmosphere of Cockney salsa. But Phil Collins doesn't lay it on the line the way Billy Joel does. You've never heard anyone quote a line from a Phil Collins song. Sure, "Take Me

Home" is a useless tune, as are "In the Air Tonight" and "One More Night." But once they end, you can barely remember what they sounded like. You can only remember that they didn't sound very good.

In summation, Phil Collins is a bald, bland Englishman who writes masses of interchangeably uninteresting songs. Like Joel, Phil Collins reached an impressive level of suckiness at an early point in his career, but unlike Joel he just stayed there. Joel moved heaven and earth to keep getting worse. Moreover, at no time in his career has Collins ever written anything as hypnotically abhorrent as "Captain Jack" or "She's Always a Woman." If I were asked to write down the names of ten Phil Collins songs that suck, I would be incapable of doing so. But I could spit out fifty Billy Joel songs right off the top of my head. In the competition for top honors between the two, I see no contest here.

Running through the entire Billy Joel and Phil Collins catalog was a good form of cultural conditioning, preparing me for the long haul ahead. By this point, I'd decided that it was time to stop listening to horrible recorded music and to go out and treat myself to some bad live material.

Luckily, Kenny G was in town.

When I showed up for Kenny G's concert at Radio City Music Hall in February 1997, I saw that I was on the right track. Gazing around at the audience—the middle-aged men in their furloughed-gangster outfits, the decrepit forty-something guys with their ELO hair—I realized that my chances of running into anybody I knew were less than zero. If I was ever forced to enter the Federal Witness Protection Program, I was simply going to tell the FBI to disguise me with some relief-pitcher hair (nothing on the sides, a mane down the back) and keep shuttling me from one Kenny G concert to another. Nobody would ever think of looking for me there. Nobody.

The concert was quite a spectacle. After Toni Braxton, the opening act, completed a long, tedious set, Kenny G, bathed in spotlights, entered from the rear of the auditorium, thereby emphasizing his solidarity with the common man. He immediately began his trademark New Age noodling, sometimes holding a single note for about two minutes. This drove the men in the crowd completely nuts—because men are impressed by other men who can sustain *anything* for more than sixty seconds. The entire time that he was playing he continued to wear the same vacant grin. Clearly, he was happy to be here. He was glad to have the work. He enjoyed the money. Yet I suspected that deep down inside, Kenny probably knew that this was not what Louis Armstrong had in mind when he institutionalized the art form known as jazz.

It has become a cliché to describe Kenny G's work as dentist's office music. But, like all clichés, there is merit in this characterization, because that is the only place people like me would usually ever hear it. And perhaps that explains why I felt such revulsion toward his work. Each of his compositions reminded me of a dental procedure I would have preferred to forget. His first number reminded me of the time I had to have braces put on my lower front teeth. His second reminded me of a double-filling day. His third reminded me of the time I didn't get my teeth cleaned for fifteen months and the technician had to scrape so hard my gums started to bleed. So maybe it wasn't the meandering, noncommittal quality of his playing or the fluffiness of his material that made me wince. Maybe I simply found Kenny G repugnant because he reminded me of going to the dentist.

As I explained in that long, overwrought section about *Cannonball Run II*, I have always had unspoken respect for things that start at a high level of horribleness and then miraculously get worse. Kenny G did not have that kind of talent. He noodled at the beginning and he noodled at the end. All of the songs were interchangeable; all of the solos were cut from the same cloth. You didn't need to sit through two hours of this stuff to get the general idea.

I bailed out of Radio City Music Hall long before Kenny G had finished his set. One reason, among many, that I left so early was my disgust at his shit-eating patter about how much he owed to his public—the mythical "you guys." His populist demeanor stood in sharp contrast to a great saxophonist like Sonny Rollins. Sonny Rollins never acts like the public has done him a favor by showing up. Sonny Rollins never dismantles the essential wall between performer and spectator. Kenny G's prancing in the aisles bleats: "I'm just like you. I'm just a lucky guy. But any one of you could be up here, too." This smarminess repelled me. If Kenny G was just an average guy with a horn, why did I have to pay $60 to see him?

Watching Kenny G reminded me that the name "Kenny" and "music" always spells disaster. Kenny G sucks. Kenny Loggins sucks. Kenny Rogers sucks. It's as if their parents studied their infant countenances and said, "Looks like he might be a musician. Let's name him Sonny or Philly Joe." But then Aunt Clara, the musician in the family, interjected, "No, he looks too mellow. Name him Kenny."

Maybe, when the three of them have grown up, they can go out on international tours, like Carreras, Domingo, and Pavarotti: *The Three Kennys in Concert*. They can even get Kenny Rankin to open for them.

Heading home from the concert, I felt deflated. An evening with Kenny G had proven to be oddly unsatisfying. It had been bad, but I'd expected it; no, I *wanted it* to be worse. Much worse.

Luckily, Barry Manilow was coming to town just a few weeks later.

Going to see Barry Manilow turned out to be one of the strangest experiences of my life. From the moment I arrived at Radio City Music Hall on April 16, 1997, I realized that this event was going to be different. When I went to see Kenny G or *Catskills on the Boardwalk* or *Cats*, I was physically repelled by most of the people in the audience, who struck me as a horde of latter-day Visigoths hell-bent on the annihilation of everything I most valued. But the Barry Manilow crowd was nothing like that. The room was filled to the rafters with wholesome young women from the outer boroughs of New York who seemed to view the singer as a sort of flamboyant younger brother who had somehow made it to the big time.

Unlike the armies of tourists who had gone to see *Cats* because that's what you do when you visit New York, or Kenny G's easy-listenin' Orks, this was an army, six thousand strong, of congenial, enthusiastic women named Vicki, every single one endowed with an adoring disposition. For the first time since I had embarked on my adventure, I did not feel physically uncomfortable in the presence of the audience. These were recognizable people, pleasant people, the kinds of affable, cheerful women who for years had been faxing my documents from Kinko's all across America.

Although I felt quite comfortable sitting among these women, I still expected to be revolted by Manilow himself. Here, I was in for my second big surprise. Manilow proved

to be an enormously likable, self-effacing, ingratiating entertainer. "What you do is not what you are," he remarked at
one point. How true. And his concert program was really
quite ingenious. Borrowing a page from Elvis Costello's mid-
eighties Broadway tour, Manilow had erected a screen behind the band with pictures of his twenty-nine album covers
flashing one at a time. Before each song, he asked an audience member to use a clicker to determine which record he
would play a selection from. They had to click fast.

To my everlasting amazement, the performances did not
turn my stomach. "This One's for You" was a winner.
"Mandy" was a delight. "Copacabana," with Rosie O'Donnell
in full Carmen Miranda regalia, brought down the house.
"Chattanooga Choo-Choo" was fantastic. "It's a Miracle,"
which ended the first set, was really and truly, a miracle.
And everyone, myself included, was overjoyed when Manilow
performed a medley of commercial jingles he had written
early in his career for State Farm, Dodge, KFC, Dr Pepper,
and McDonald's.

"Have it your way," Barry sang cheerfully.

No, Barry, have it your way.

At intermission, I had to step outside to gather my wits.
Was I simply pretending to have a good time because I didn't
want the plump young woman sitting next to me to feel bad?
No, that wouldn't have been like me, for I am, and always have
been, a prick. Was I growing nostalgic for the seventies? Unlikely—Nixon, Carter, Andy Gibb. Or was I gradually losing
my mind? At first, I decided that the answer must be a mixture
of all three. Though mostly the third explanation. Not until
the second half of the show was under way did I realize why I
had succumbed to the allure of a musician I had once associated with everything I despised in American popular music.

Barry Manilow was a has-been.

It was Manilow himself who provided this insight about halfway through the second set. Looking on in perhaps rehearsed, but nonetheless wide-eyed disbelief at the enthusiastic way the crowd responded to numbers like "I Write the Songs" and "Can't Smile Without You," Manilow expressed his heartfelt gratitude to the crowd, because they still came out to see him whenever he blew through town. After all, he noted, "I haven't had a hit in fifteen years. I've never been on MTV. But you're still here."

Here, Manilow had cut through to the crux of the onion ring. Sure, Manilow could still sell out Radio City Music Hall for a week. Sure, he could still pull in the crowds at music fairs all over the hinterland. But the days at Madison Square Garden were over. And yet, he soldiered on. And that was the secret to his appeal. At least to me. For there is nothing in the annals of show business more heartwarming than the saga of the aging trouper.

But from my perspective there was another factor at work. I had long subscribed to the theory that if an entertainer who is the apotheosis of Pure Evil hangs around long enough, even people like me will eventually develop a grudging affection for them. Partially, this is because once they are no longer ubiquitous superstars, they have in some way been defanged. They are no longer a menace, and can be enjoyed as pure, unadulterated kitsch.

I knew that this was true because of my Jerry Lewis experience. Eight months before I saw Barry Manilow, I bought tickets to see Jerry Lewis in *Damn Yankees*. Throughout most of my life, Jerry Lewis had embodied the most hateful features of show biz: cheeseball glitz, a galling mixture of false modesty, colossal egotism, and overall schmuckiness. That started to change with his glorious turn in Martin Scorsese's brilliant *The King of Comedy*. Now, after all these years, it was possible to see him for what he was: an old trouper. Breathes there a man with soul so dead he never to himself has said: Yea, verily, I am touched by the lion in winter's final victory lap?

I think not. I think very not.

As Lewis strode toward the spotlights at the end of the show, I was the first person out of my seat to applaud him. My daughter, unaccustomed to such spontaneous bursts of emotion, could not help commenting upon my unexpected élan.

"Boy, Dad, you must really like this guy," she said.

I smiled, as we gathered our coats and programs.

"It's complicated, Bridget," I said. "I'll explain it when you're older."

When I saw Barry Manilow, I had exactly the same experience. Here was a guy who knew how to put on a show. Not a show I necessarily wanted to see, but a show all the same. Here was a guy who understood that no performance was complete without dragging some woman who had flown all the way from England up onto the stage for a kiss and a cuddle. Here was a guy who realized that when the public had given so much, you had to give something back. Here was a guy who knew that when six thousand women named Debbie get together with one guy named Barry, there's going to be magic in the moonlight.

I am certainly not suggesting that after all these years in the business, Barry Manilow had finally learned to sing or dance, or that his songs had miraculously stopped sucking. "I Write the Songs" was still a crime against nature. Manilow still danced like a spindly Travolta impersonator. And the guy who writes the songs that made the whole world sing still sang like Barry Manilow. I am only saying that his songs were at least songs, not pointless New Age riffing like Kenny G's interminable jerking off. And unlike Billy Joel or Phil Collins,

Manilow seemed to be doing material that he genuinely believed in, songs that were appropriate for his personality. "Memory" may have been pure schmaltz, but Manilow was nothing if not a schmaltzmeister. Like Lawrence Welk or Liberace before him, he knew himself and he knew his audience. My hat was off to him.

One final note: While I do believe that if an entertainer who is the apotheosis of Pure Evil hangs around long enough, even people like me will eventually develop a grudging affection for them, I can say, without fear of being contradicted, that this theory would not have applied to Sammy Davis, Jr.

For several weeks after seeing Kenny G and Barry Manilow, I felt starved for bad live music. Foolishly, I had missed a chance to see Yanni at the Foxwoods Casino in northern Connecticut. But I did go out and buy a couple of his records. Once again, I was crushed by the experience. Yanni definitely fell into the category of things that didn't reek nearly as much as I would have liked them to. Although we had inhabited the same solar system for some time, I had no idea what his music was like until I purchased *In the Mirror,* "a collection of Yanni favorites, including a special version of 'Aria' from *Live at the Acropolis*." As it turned out, this was the only tune I recognized. Generally, I found his music bland but inoffensive. Often, it sounded like the kind of generic disco music that was played in Eastern European cabarets just before the Berlin Wall fell. Other songs, with titles like "Forbidden Dreams," "Face in the Photograph," and "So Long, My Friend" sounded like Spanish music sung the way Greeks must have imagined it. In general, the wistful ballads seemed to express the heartfelt yearnings of decent human beings who probably scored less than one thousand on their SATs. Frequently, on tracks like "One Man's Dream," it sounded like the piano music they play in French movies of the 1970s, where Alain Delon finally realizes that Nathalie Baye doesn't love him anymore.

One day, while trawling for twaddle, I stumbled upon an unexpectedly rich source of middlebrow hokum: those infuriating PBS fund-raisers, where a cabal of bespectacled dweebs try to convince you that the only thing that stands between Newt Gingrich and the eclipse of Western civilization as we know it is your viewer dollars. Then they return to the extraordinary fare that can be found only on public television: Patti LuPone warbling a few selections from *Evita*; Peter, Paul & Mary reliving that march on Selma; a bracing evening of Celtic hopscotch with *Lord of the Lap Dance*'s Michael Flatley dolled up in that puffy shirt from "Seinfeld."

Yet it was through PBS that I was exposed to the seminal bad musical experience of my entire self-immersion in America's cultural hot zone. That was the night I watched "John Tesh: The Avalon Concert." Everyone knows that John Tesh makes Kenny G sound like Andres Segovia, but this in itself is not a crime. What is a crime is the use of taxpayer dollars to subsidize his peculiar career. Public television was originally supposed to bring the public educational programming and cultural fare that was not widely available otherwise. But John Tesh's music can be heard in elevators everywhere.

There is something dispiriting about watching this blow-dried oaf preening on these putatively cerebral fund-raisers. Tesh, who aspires to a kind of early seventies hipness, with stage mannerisms borrowed from Tom Jones, is living proof that the human capacity for self-deception, long thought to be vast, is in fact infinite. In the late 1970s, legend has it,

Howard Cosell came into possession of classified documents revealing that he was the biggest schmuck in the lower forty-eight and that everyone hated him. It was too late in his career to do anything with this information; like a golfer with a tendency to hook the ball, Cosell could not at this late date reverse years of sucking and suddenly become an acceptable human being. But at least he did not go to his grave thinking people liked him. He did not go to meet his Maker oblivious to the truth about himself.

Alas, I think John Tesh will. Though Jay Leno burns his CDs on the "Tonight" show, though Buffy the Vampire Slayer identifies Tesh as Satan, though an entire nation has come to use the words *Tesh* and *lame* interchangeably, one senses in watching him perform that he is unaware of the immense ill will he generates. He is almost supernaturally vacant.

One thing that did impress me about John Tesh in his TV concert was the meticulous attention he had devoted to detail, taking great pains to ensure that he had not left out one revolting cliché or infuriating tic. It was as if he knew that his enemies were out there and wanted to make sure that the night was extra-excruciating. First, the camera panned down the rocky coast past the waves breaking on the shore as a tingling piano played in the background. Then, the entrance from the rear, the high-fiving of the audience, the whole Aw Shucks routine, followed by the lullaby for his daughter, the acoustic tribute to the mountain, and the fab guitarist, cutting-edge bassist, and Gypsy violinist joining him at the side of the piano for a heavy-duty rave-up.

If this kind of programming was going to be the norm during pledge week, it was time for PBS to stop giving away tote bags and start thinking about complimentary barf bags.

Scant days after I watched the PBS fund-raiser, I learned that Tesh would be appearing in concert at Carnegie Hall a few weeks later. I bought my tickets the morning they went on sale and began the nervous wait for the big day. Finally, the night arrived. It does Tesh no disservice to say that there was a noticeable lack of electricity in the concert hall before showtime. Carnegie Hall holds 2,800 people, but ushers assured me that Tesh had sold only 1,100 tickets. There were many, many empty seats in the upper regions of the hall, and I strongly suspected that Tesh had papered the room to make his Carnegie Hall debut seem more impressive. It was sadder than sad.

As I waited for Tesh to take the stage, I felt an engulfing sense of dread. There were far too many families, far too many geeky guys in herringbone jackets, far too much plaid. This was not a Carnegie Hall–type crowd. This was a crowd of Philistines on an overnight trip from Gaza who had come to Jerusalem to profane the temple. In the twenty-one years that I had lived in New York, I had seen Arthur Rubinstein, Maurizio Pollini, Herbert von Karajan, Alfred Brendel, Bill Monroe and the Bluegrass Boys, and the Chieftains on this stage. All these musicians got to Carnegie Hall by practicing. None of them got there by being the host of "Entertainment Tonight." Tesh's presence in the hall was tantamount to a blue-eyed infidel invading the Great Mosque of Mecca. It was a crime against both God and man. This man. Yet I was enthralled, curious to see if Tesh in person could attain the Olympian heights of suckiness he had already reached on his records and television specials.

About ten minutes after eight, the lights finally went down and the band surged onto the stage. I knew I was in for a long night when a low-rent light show started to blaze across the concert hall and a disembodied voice invoked the legend of Avalon. Culturally speaking, anything involving the Knights of the Round Table usually signifies big-time flatulence up ahead. The only thing potentially more discouraging would have involved whales.

When the Arthurian hokum finally petered out, the band launched into some weird, New Age, quasi-Caribbean riffing—Cornhusker Flamenco. As the lights continued their assault on the audience, Tesh himself appeared at center stage, spasmodically gesturing toward the members of his band. (Tesh is much given to tired, hackneyed, neo-Stallonian gestures such as thrusting his fists into the air to signify a triumph he has not in fact achieved.)

Finally, he hunkered down at the piano and the concert formally began. Now things got really unpleasant. With his shopworn, lounge-lizard stage gestures, eviscerated salsa compositions, and studied reveries, Tesh was a human Cuisinart of every hack musical stunt, effecting a strange synthesis of various mongrel styles where half the songs sounded like generic background music for promotional videos (*Dayton, Ohio—On the Move!*) and the other half sounded like retreads of Mason Williams's sixties hit "Classical Gas." Tonight, before he had come on stage, Tesh had clearly made a mental checklist of every musical cliché of the past thirty years. Arthurian mystery. Check. Inexpensive light show. Check. Goatee. Check. Gypsy violinist in military jacket dropping to his knees. Check. Paisley vest. Check. Conga solo. Check. Sideman with the worst case of guitar face this side of G. E. Smith. Check.

It was a night I would not soon forget. Seeing John Tesh parade around a stage customarily occupied by titans like Vladimir Horowitz and Georg Solti was like looking at those old black-and-white photos of Adolf Hitler preening in the shadow of the Eiffel Tower.

Say what you will, Hitler had better taste in music.

The Mistake by the Lake

*O*ne question that begs asking is how often in the course of my investigations I came upon something that was not anywhere near as horrible as I had expected it to be, or, *mirabile dictu,* was not horrible at all? Well, for starters, there was Barry Manilow. And there was also the all-you-can-eat salad bar at the Sizzler, which was much better than I had been led to believe. But what was more impressive still was the proletarian charm of this unabashedly downscale dining establishment, which stood in charming contrast to the coy ambience of a Red Lobster or the counterfeit mariachi atmosphere of a Taco Bell. Inexpensive, plentiful, and, with the exception of the pallid Malibu Chicken, surprisingly edible, the Sizzler was a big hit with my family, and particularly with my two children, who were fast tiring of impaling themselves on Dad's Catherine wheel of mordant irony.

Perhaps the best thing about the nearby Sizzler I visited on three different occasions was the enthusiastic demeanor of the Ivory Coast waiters who brought the drinks to our table. Hardworking immigrants with no pretensions to being actors, dancers, stand-up comics, or fledgling rock stars, no bushy ponytails, no attitudes, no primal need to commend the patron on his or her choice of the sixteen-ounce steak as opposed to the ten-ounce hamburger, these affable young men made my visits to the Sizzler an absolute delight. I do not think it is going too far to say that the Sizzler, like Bob's Big Boy, serves as an eloquent symbol for all that is best about America—cheap food, and lots of it—and that if we had only invited the Soviet Politburo to sample the joys of these chains several decades ago, the Cold War would have ended by the 1970s. A visitor from a second- or third-world country need gaze only once at the Appetizers Bar at either of these chains to realize the awesome truth: America wins, on points.

What were some of the other surprises that lay in store for me? Well, Martin Cruz Smith and Ken Follett both turned out to be much better writers than I had ever thought possible. For virtually my entire adult life *Gorky Park* and *Eye of the Needle* had been staring up at me from bookstore displays and used-book kiosks, but I had always assumed that anything this popular had to be at least as inane as *The Bourne Identity*, *The Icarus Agenda*, *The Bucephalus Paradigm*, or *The Priapus Contingency*. But when I actually sat down to read *Gorky Park*, a murder mystery set in Moscow focusing on the international sable-smuggling underworld, it turned out to be a beautifully crafted, thoroughly fascinating page-turner. To a lesser extent, this was also true of *Eye of the Needle*, which I finally got around to reading one rainy April morning while my daughter was having surgery to repair a broken ankle. Frankly, I was flabbergasted by its abundant merits. I couldn't put the little sucker down.

One thought that stayed with me long after I had finished reading this ripping yarn about high-stakes espionage in the days leading up to D-Day was the passage on page 226 where the Nazi spy who is the novel's main character unexpectedly goes down on the demure heroine:

"He slipped down the bed, between her thighs, and kissed her belly. His tongue flicked in and out of her navel. It felt quite nice, she thought. His head went lower. Surely he doesn't want to kiss me *there*. He did. And he did more than kiss. His lips pulled at the soft folds of her skin. She was paralyzed by shock as his tongue began to probe in the crevices and then, as he parted her lips with his fingers, to thrust deep inside her . . ."

This passage is relevant for a number of reasons. First, it is the sort of material that should be studied carefully by the legions of romance writers who have gotten into the annoying habit of talking about how Ariadne's lover Slade Kincaid instructed her in a thousand different lovemaking positions without ever going into details about a single one of them. Ladies, forget about the Kama Sutra and all that mystical Eastern balderdash. Forget about the 1,001 positions of love. The only thing your readers are interested in is getting their husbands or boyfriends to go down on them. Walk into any CVS in America and study the facial expressions on the women who buy all those *Love's Buffed Cuirass*—type books. You're not going to find women who want to read about the 1,001 positions of love, but housewives who'd like to read about some good, old-fashioned, super-hot muff diving. They've long since given up on persuading Herb or Mikey to make love to them while suspended from an oak tree. They don't care about Herb or Mikey making love to them on the desktop while Vaseline-lubricated FAX paper snakes through their undulating thighs. They'd just like Herb or Mikey to go down on them for once in their lives.

The passage is of interest for one other reason. Perhaps

because I was raised by Jesuits, I had long believed that cunnilingus was a sexual technique that only gained widespread popularity in the 1960s and 1970s, and was never, ever practiced by members of my parents' generation, who would have found it disconcertingly non–Andrews Sisterish, if not completely gross. Moreover, I was fully persuaded that cunnilingus had *never* been practiced in the British Isles while Churchill was alive; it just didn't seem like the sort of thing you would associate with Mrs. Miniver or Mr. Chips, much less Dame Judith Anderson or Alec Guinness. Last but not least, I found it amazing that cunnilingus would be practiced—even in a fictional setting—by a Nazi spy, because Nazis never seemed like the sort of people who would go out of their way to pleasure their partners. For this and many other reasons, *Eye of the Needle* was an absolute eye-opener for me, just going to show, once again, how wrong you can be about some things.

Were there any other instances where my deeply held prejudices were proven to be utterly unfounded? Yes, after I finished hacking my way through the March 1997 CVS bestseller list, which included everything from Fran Drescher's *Enter Whining* to Danielle Steel's *Five Days in Paris*, John Grisham read like Marcel Proust. And Whoopi Goldberg's performance in *A Funny Thing Happened on the Way to the Forum* was also just swell. A veteran of innumerable bad movies, Goldberg had always impressed me as a sort of Nubian Chevy Chase: someone who once may have been funny, but who had long since lost the plot and now had no way of finding her way back because she was surrounded by fawning minions too stupid or cowed to break the news to her that she was revolting.

It was her revolting work that I was thinking of when I bought my tickets for *Forum*, work like *Eddie, Jumpin' Jack*

Flash, *Corrina, Corrina*, and *Boys on the Side*. I was ready for some big-time sucking, and I was sure that Whoopi could provide it.

But Whoopi threw me a curve with her performance. For the first time in recent memory she was cast in the right role, as a clownish ringmaster, a lovable jerk. The role played to her strengths. She mugged. She did outrageous double takes. She ad-libbed. She teased latecomers. She sold the merchandise. Naturally, she overstayed her welcome at the end by browbeating the audience into contributing to her favorite charity (AIDS, what else?), fulfilling the contemporary celebrity's sacred mission of never failing to remind people from rural Ohio that it is Los Angelenos, not itinerant Buckeyes, who occupy the moral high ground in this country. But as a performer, she was an absolute peach.

After I saw *Forum*, I mentioned to a couple of friends that it was the first time I had ever seen Whoopi Goldberg in something that made me laugh. They both said, "Hey, what about *Ghost*?" I replied that I had never seen *Ghost*. They told me that this was a big mistake. I found this hard to believe, but just to be on the safe side, I rented the film that evening. My God, how right they were! *Ghost*, it will be recalled, is the surprise 1990 hit in which Patrick Swayze is murdered by his best friend and then spends the rest of the movie trying to warn his old girlfriend, Demi Moore, that her life is in danger. He is assisted in this effort by the redoubtable Whoopi, who plays a crooked spiritualist. The film was a garden of unexpected pleasures.

For starters, there was Whoopi's stirring, punitive rendition of "I'm Henry the Eighth," used as a weapon to get Swayze to leave her apartment. Then there were the bargain-basement monsters who swarmed all over the villain at the end of the movie. Finally, there was Demi Moore's valiant attempt to act. But there was also an amazing scene where Swayze, desperate to establish posthumous contact with his old flame, slips into Whoopi's body and starts to dance with Demi. The only thing that prevented this scene from going down in cinema history as a rival to Rhett's staircase farewell to Scarlett O'Hara was Whoopi's inexplicable failure to kiss Demi, for then we would have had a double-header: some interracial romance from beyond the grave, plus a little lesbo action on the side. Alas, you can't have everything.

My favorite part of the film was the scene in the very beginning where Swayze gets murdered and a second, spectral Patrick Swayze appears at his side. This seemed preposterously cheeky on the part of the director, as if he was taunting the audience: "If you think Patrick Swayze is a bad actor when he's alive, wait till you see him when he's dead." And it was an amazingly prophetic scene, because it brilliantly anticipated the cloning controversy a full seven years before Scottish scientist Ian Wilmut successfully cloned Dolly the Sheep. For it is the moment when two Patrick Swayzes appear on the screen at one and the same time that the audience is confronted with the most powerful argument against cloning ever devised. The world can easily survive the cloning of 2 Adolf Hitlers, 5 Idi Amins, 119 Saddam Husseins. It is the possibility of a second Patrick Swayze or a third Barbra Streisand that should have us all quaking in our boots.

An even scarier thought occurs late in the movie when an invisible Swayze confronts the villain. What's remarkable is that Swayze does his best acting while completely invisible. Which again brings us to the question of cloning: If you think that one Patrick Swayze you can actually see is frightening, how about two Patrick Swayzes that you can't?

But perhaps the biggest surprise of all occurred when I made a three-day pilgrimage to the Mistake by the Lake. One Sunday afternoon in February 1997, I tuned in the NBA All-Star Game, which was being played in Cleveland, Ohio. Perennial All-Star and Highlight Film Choker Karl Malone had raised a few hackles earlier in the weekend by questioning the NBA's decision to hold the All-Star Game in such a charmless backwater. As I watched the game, I mentioned to my wife that Cleveland had always been blighted with a reputation as a place that really bit the big one, so maybe I should add it to my must-see list.

By a weird coincidence, I received a phone call the very next day from a representative of the Cleveland Film Festival, who asked if I would like to attend the twenty-first annual gathering of Buckeye film buffs and deliver a speech about my valiant but doomed 1994 low-budget film *12 Steps to Death*. A few weeks later, I found myself at the Renaissance Hotel in downtown Cleveland. The experience was a revelation. Though eerily quiet after sundown, with a downtown area that made Philadelphia's Center City seem like Gay Paree, Cleveland was a thoroughly entertaining little burgh. A fantastic art museum. A beautiful, human-scale ballpark. The most gorgeous concert hall I had seen anywhere in these United States. A city teeming with die-hard football fans. A booming little pseudo-Soho called the Flats. Good restaurants. A perfectly acceptable level of nightlife. A splendid country-and-western radio station. Most important of all, a genuinely friendly citizenry.

Of course, my perception *was* somewhat colored by the fact that I was being treated like visiting royalty by my hosts at the Cleveland Film Festival. But I'd been treated like visiting royalty by my hosts in places like Raleigh-Durham, North Carolina, and Dallas, Texas, and had still come away with the impression that they were cultural tar pits, if not flat-out dumps. So I did not think I was being taken for a ride here.

One thing that I liked about the cadre of young film buffs who squired me around Cleveland was their attitude toward the Rock 'n' Roll Hall of Fame. Almost without exception, they realized that the very idea of institutionalizing rock 'n' roll was a cheap stunt cooked up by the City Fathers to boost tourism. For one, rock 'n' roll hadn't been around long enough to deserve a Hall of Fame. Two, the Turtles were in it. Three, Cleveland did not have a legitimate claim to the role of Rock Mecca, ceding pride of place to Memphis, New York, Los Angeles, San Francisco, and Philadelphia, not to mention London, England. Four, the Turtles were in it. Five, the Hall of Fame seemed to attract enormous throngs of RVers and organized school groups of acne-ravaged schoolkids who had no bona fide connection with the idiom. Last but not least, the Turtles were in it.

For a number of reasons other than the Turtles' inclusion, the Rock 'n' Roll Hall of Fame didn't quite measure up. For starters, the building itself suffered from the Guggenheim syndrome: the aggressively futuristic architecture made the contents of the museum seem irrelevant. Second, the museum was too cool to be in Cleveland, which, for all its efforts to spruce itself up, was still a pretty dowdy place. The weird juxtaposition of I. M. Pei's space-age building with Cleveland's otherwise stolid downtown architecture reminded me of the foolish decision the city of Philadelphia made a few years back when it allowed a gigantic metallic clothespin by Claes Oldenburg to be erected right across the street from the City of Brotherly Love's eye-catching but hideous City Hall, a late-nineteenth-century neo-Gothic monstrosity. Such attempts to manufacture a superficial aura of cutting-edge hipness were a cheap, sleight-of-hand trick, like Harley-straddling dentists in Litchfield, Connecticut, sporting doo rags and Ray-Bans.

The Hall of Fame interior was exactly like all those ferociously pedagogic science museums that have sprung up across America in the past ten years, only without the science. One interactive exhibit explained that the two principal influences on Jim Morrison were Willie Dixon, composer of "Backdoor Man," and Kurt Weill, who wrote "Alabama Song." (I would challenge this position, arguing that the two principal influences on Jim Morrison were vermouth and nicotine, with maybe a bit of lysergic acid diethylamide thrown in for good measure.)

A big problem with the Rock 'n' Roll Hall of Fame—and with most American museums of any historical genre—was that the permanent collection didn't exactly knock anybody's socks off. That's because none of the objects on display had been around long enough to impress anybody other than senescent RVers and prepubescent school groups. Go visit the British Museum in Merrie Olde England and you can see the Magna Carta. Go visit the Louvre in Paris and you can see the *Venus de Milo*. Go visit Independence Hall in Philadelphia and you can see the Liberty Bell. Somehow, Madonna's brassiere and Paul Simon's handwritten notes for "The Sounds of Silence" don't pack quite the same wallop.

My reaction to the Rock 'n' Roll Hall of Fame was identical to my experience when I ate at the original Hard Rock Café in Los Angeles two weeks later. One half of the restaurant was dedicated to Jimi Hendrix, Bob Dylan, John Lennon, the Stones, Elvis. That's not where I was seated. Since I was dining alone, and didn't look like anybody special, I was banished to a table all the way over on the other side of the room, directly under an exhibit that consisted of guitars belonging to Lenny Kravitz, Seal, Jakob Dylan, and the Foo Fighters. It's as if the staff had sized me up as soon as I came in and decided I wasn't cool enough to be in the Bob Dylan section. No sooner had I crossed the threshold than the Hard Rock cafeteria crew had me pegged as a Wallflowers kind of guy.

Suffering through an unsuccessful meal of bland chili and hopeless pork ribs, I couldn't help feeling sorry for the army of Hispanic cooks behind the bar who had to stand there all day making culturally incongruous Po' Boys while listening to Bob Seger's "Against the Wind." Surely, they hadn't risked death in crossing the Rio Grande for this.

Eventually, I noticed that I was seated directly under a tennis dress worn by one Dolores O'Riordan. Who on earth was Dolores O'Riordan? I asked my waitress. She's the lead singer from the Cranberries, I was told. I knew the Cranberries; I had two of their records. They seemed like a competent little combo. But I was astonished that a band with a catalog so minuscule and a mythology so picayune was already being immortalized. Putting the lead singer from the Cranberries on a wall inside the original Hard Rock Café seemed a lot like putting the lead singer from the Raspberries on a wall inside the Rock 'n' Roll Hall of Fame.

Come to think of it, the lead singer from the Raspberries *had been* immortalized on a wall in the Rock 'n' Roll Hall of Fame—Eric Carmen hails from Cleveland, and is one of the linchpins of the museum's fanciful second-story exhibit, where the great city of Cleveland makes its rather spurious claim to the title of "the heart of rock 'n' roll." During his brief career, Carmen sang such hits as "Go All the Way" and "All by Myself." This ain't rock 'n' roll. This is genocide.

Another dud element in the permanent collection of the Rock 'n' Roll Hall of Fame was the exhibit of rock star memorabilia. Jimi Hendrix's Stratocasters didn't look much different from the Stratocasters you could see in any music store in any town in America. And because rock 'n' roll is a musical idiom that devours its own young, the silly outfits that the Beatles wore in 1964 didn't look any sillier than the outfits Michael Jackson wore in 1993. As for that Plasmatics exhibit, putting anything that those jokers wore in the Hall of Fame was like retiring Mitch Williams's number and shipping his uniform straight to Cooperstown. Sure, all of these folks played in the big leagues for a few years. But they didn't put up the numbers.

Still, I was not willing to allow my disappointment with Cleveland's No. 1 tourist attraction to cloud my generally positive view of the city. Like Baltimore and Philadelphia, it was a once-mighty American city that had fallen on hard times and was now making a concerted effort to pick itself up off the canvas and return to its former glory. Unlike Baltimore, a slum with a nice baseball stadium and a large aquarium, Cleveland seemed to be managing the transformation. At a time when so many Americans were fleeing to cultural wastelands like the cities trumpeted in *Money* magazine's annual Best Places to Live survey, Cleveland served as a potent reminder that there are certain resources that only great cities can offer. Professional baseball. Great symphony orchestras. Van Goghs. Most important of all, fans who die a thousand deaths when the pro football club up and leaves town. Fans who die a thousand deaths watching their teams suffer through decades of abject failure are the people who make America great.

Perhaps the greatest homage I can pay to the much-maligned Mistake by the Lake is that the whole time I was in Cleveland, I met only one person I did not like. Needless to say, he was a waiter in an upscale eatery, described by my hosts as the finest restaurant in the city. Needless to say, he had a ponytail. Needless to say, he had an attitude. Needless to say, he continually interrupted the conversation to make sure everything was all right. Needless to say, he commended certain patrons for their dining choices, but glowered at me for ordering my steak well done. His demeanor reminded me of the time an old friend described *Vanity Fair* as a magazine that was read by every cool waiter in St. Louis. Obviously, Cleveland was also groaning under the cruel satrapy of the hep waitstaff.

At the conclusion of our meal, the waiter asked if I would be having dessert. I said that I would not. He told me—and this is a direct quote—that I "would be making a great mistake if I didn't sample some of the restaurant's desserts," adding, "We have the best tiramisu in Cleveland."

I found this remark radiantly bizarre. By declaring that the restaurant offered the best tiramisu in Cleveland, my waiter seemed to hold open the possibility that a slightly better brand of tiramisu could be found downstate in Cincinnati, or perhaps at some superb eatery named Le Chat Qui Pêche in Columbus, Ohio. Why he did not simply go for broke and proclaim, "We have the best tiramisu in Ohio!" or "We have the best tiramisu in the whole goddamn Rust

Belt!" is beyond me; it wasn't as if I was going to go out and check.

As I exited the restaurant, chastened and dessertless, I thought back to my dining experiences with Moussa, my Sierra Leonean waiter at the Sizzler. Ponytail-less, attitudeless, bouyant, noncondescending, Moussa would never have dared upbraid me for my failure to visit the Sizzler's legendary Dessert Bar. It occurred to me that if restaurants all across America would merely purge their staffs of would-be actors sporting ponytails and replace them with intrepid immigrants who actually knew their ass from third base, this would once again be a sane and healthy nation.

But one brain-dead waiter was not enough to spoil my visit to the unfairly titled Mistake by the Lake.

Not even the Turtles could do that.

Iowa on the Hudson

*I*n the winter of 1997, I compiled a list of all the explicitly horrible plays that were running on Broadway, then systematically began working my way through them. I had several good reasons for doing this. For some time, I'd been noticing that inferior entertainment was starting to have a hypnotic effect on my personality. Back when I'd launched myself on this descent into the abyss, I could easily shift gears and go to see something uplifting and entertaining, like John Osborne's *The Entertainer*, Jerome Kern and Oscar Hammerstein II's *Show Boat*, or Bill Irwin's production of Molière's *Scapin*, then turn around the next day and subject myself to *Phantom*.

It wasn't until I attended a performance of *Chicago* at Christmastime that I realized how much my multifaceted cultural hegira was taking over my life. *Chicago* was a miracle by the standards of contemporary Broadway: acerbic, intelligent, well-acted, with fantastic music and astonishing dancing. But by this point, after so many bad books, so many bad movies, so many bad concerts, my nervous system was no longer responding well to intelligent, sophisticated enter-tainment. I was fast becoming addicted to twaddle.

This being the case, I began haunting the Great White Way, taking in every truckload of piffle available. But once again, the *scheissenbedauern* phenomenon reared its ugly head, as I found myself continually disappointed by the crap-piness of the crap I saw. Most Broadway musicals are bad, but they are bad in a safe, predictable way. *The Phantom of the Opera* is a big, corny operetta with lots of terrible num-bers, the kind of musical where the sets elicit more applause than the cast, as well they should. But it's not bad in the apocalyptic way that *Cats* is bad. Nor is *Les Miserables*. It's true that *Les Miserables* has only one good song ("Master of the House"), but frankly, by Broadway standards, that's a lot. Indeed, the most appalling thing about attending a perfor-mance of *Les Miz* was not the musical itself but the spectacle of seeing a roomful of middle-Americans get all weepy-eyed about the plight of desperately poor French people and the inequities of a judicial system that would hound a man to his grave for the mere crime of stealing a loaf of bread. Middle-Americans hate poor people, loathe the French, and are forever electing public officials who make it their life's work to put the wretched of the earth in the slammer for stealing a loaf of bread. This being the case, the audience's crocodile tears did not weep true.

Sunset Boulevard also fell into that gray area between cow dung and hogwash. By the time I got to see *Sunset Boul-evard,* it was working on its third or fourth star and heading for its final curtain in about ten days. Elaine Page, a solid old British warhorse, was still doing a creditable job in the role of Norma Desmond, but the audience, which had come en masse all the way in from the amber waves of grain, made no real effort to clasp her to its bosom. *Sunset Boulevard* is the type of show that must have a big star like Glenn Close to succeed, because the audience at some level suspects that what happened to Gloria Swanson and what happened to Norma Desmond may one day happen to Close, when she can no longer land starring roles in movies like *Mars Attacks* and *101 Dalmatians,* and they kind of like that. But the audience could care less what happens to the careers of Betty Buckley or Elaine Page; for all they know, it may have already happened.

There are no good songs in *Sunset Boulevard*, no "Memory," no "Music of the Night," *nothing.* Suffering through it, I realized that the musical was a victim of its own weird subtext: a British star nobody had ever heard of was being asked to play a washed-up, American silent-film star nobody had ever heard of in a theater that was only half-filled because the star that everybody had heard of had jumped ship a year earlier and everybody had already seen the movie anyway. Intentionally or not, the show had the smell of death about it. In fact, it had the smell of numerous deaths.

Miss Saigon, like *Sunset Boulevard,* was the type of lavish production where the sets, and most particularly the life-size, cheesy-looking helicopter that lands on the stage in Act II, evoke more applause than the performers, as well they should. Like *Les Miserables,* the musical is a cynical attempt to transmute dire human misfortune into a commodity for the amusement of the gentry. Nobody in the audience really cares about all those little Asian-American tykes who were left behind after the war in Vietnam, any more than they care about all those disenfranchised nineteenth-century French peasants in *Les Miz.* Least of all me. None of this would have been a problem if the show had any great songs in it. It did not.

The one valuable lesson I learned while haunting the

highways and byways of the Great White Way was that even if you're trapped inside a theater for several hours listening to some desiccated floozie caterwauling about an industry that has no use for aging actresses, it is still possible to use your time constructively. When I saw *Miss Saigon*, I quickly tired of hearing an Asian-American actress who is supposed to be a doomed Vietnamese hooker singing in the same namby-pamby voice as the little girl in *Annie*. So I decided to go downstairs and make some important phone calls. But then I remembered that big helicopter scene, which I was loathe to miss out on. So I cornered an usherette and offered her $5 to come down and retrieve me when the helicopter finally landed. This she was more than happy to do.

In the long run, I think this could be a very effective way for usherettes to supplement their income: by offering to wake up theatergoers for the good songs or scenes in exchange for a nominal sum of money. You could have the usherettes at *Cats* alerting you when Grizabella sings "Memory," the usherettes at *Phantom* calling you back upstairs when the theater's most famous burn victim belts out "The Music of the Night," and the usherettes at *Titanic* summoning you to your seat when that massive floating city finally plummets to its briny grave. A terrific revenue-generating scheme, if I say so myself.

Titanic was another example of a musical that did not chomp anywhere near as much as I would have liked it to. Though the show had no memorable numbers, the score was dignified and functional, and the staging of the play was actually quite interesting. I saw the musical shortly after it opened, when there was still some question as to whether the equipment to make the ship sink would actually work, and uncharacteristically, I shelled out $150 for two tickets in the second row. Lots of people have theorized about the enduring, generations-spanning appeal of the *Titanic* myth. Some say that the tragedy continues to fascinate the public because it illustrates our fragility in the face of a vindictive God; others are riveted by the class-warfare element, since the rich passengers basically screwed the Irish immigrants in steerage; still others are mesmerized by the grace-under-fire subtext, with some women refusing to leave the boat without their husbands.

But as I watched the ship capsize, as the doomed passengers dragged themselves up the gangway, hoping to buy a few minutes' respite before going quietly into that good night, I realized that for me the appeal of the story was much more primal. I wanted to see that big sucker go down. I'd sat there for two and a half hours (the play lasted longer than the ship) watching those *über*-WASP dinks take their afternoon tea and smoke their huge cigars and for some unfathomable reason that probably has a lot to do with having grandparents from County Cork, I wanted to see the whole lot of them drown. I did feel bad for the Celts in steerage, but looking on the bright side, hurtling to the bottom of the ocean was still probably a whole lot more fun than any of them were going to have if they'd stayed in Ireland.

As I've said before, once you've set out on the trail of a hideous wild boar, gunning down a doddering old stag is not the way you want to come back to the hunting lodge. Thus, even though I was flabbergasted to find that, like *Titanic*, *The King and I* and *Annie* were perfectly acceptable, professional productions, they were not what I was in the market for. Increasingly, my scope of interest was narrowing to the point that it only included things that blew it right out the ass. I wanted to stare directly into the eye of the tiger while standing on the deck of a hurricane-swept four-rigger and barf my guts out till the sun shined, Nellie. It was inevitable, therefore, that I should find myself, in the late spring of 1997, at a Wednesday matinee of *Grease*.

I have never, ever understood the *Grease* phenomenon. Born in 1950, I can vividly recall the 1950s exactly the way they were: putrid. Americans love to look back on the 1950s as an earlier, more innocent time, but I seem to recall little items like the McCarthy era, the development of the H-bomb, the Korean War, and one hell of a lot of black people hanging from trees. True, there was some great music—Elvis, Chuck Berry, Roy Orbison, Carl Perkins, Jerry Lee Lewis—but you don't hear anything that resembles their material in *Grease*. The music in *Grease* is solid, unadulterated doo-wop, precisely the kind of carcinogenic horseshit that the British Invasion purged from the charts in 1964. Thanks again, Fab Four. We owe you one.

By the time I saw *Grease* in 1997, it was farther removed in time from the original production of the show than the original production of the show was removed in time from the era it portrayed. In this sense, the show did not hark back to an earlier, more innocent time when Dwight D. Eisenhower was president, but to an earlier, more innocent time when Gerald Ford was president. Or maybe it was Jimmy Carter. Either way, bad karma. In fact, the good will that the public continues to feel toward the show probably has less to do with affection for the fifties than with affection for the young John Travolta and the intermittently talented

Olivia Newton-John. But John Travolta and Olivia Newton-John weren't in the show the day I saw it.

The day I saw it, the producers were resorting to low-grade stunts to pull the rubes into the theater. Ads in the *New York Times* proclaimed that Joe Piscopo was the new star of the show, ably supported by Dominique Dawes, the prettiest but least effective member of the 1996 U.S. Olympic gold medal–winning Women's Gymastics Team. This is about as close as you can get to misleading advertising without getting yourself tossed into the calaboose. Piscopo had a bit part in the production, playing a deejay who occasionally popped out of a hole at the top of the stage to holler something vaguely hepcattish. And Dawes did a couple of handstands but had almost no dialogue.

Grease was one of those shows that made you realize why Broadway has fast become Iowa-on-the-Hudson. An endless parade of fart jokes, cigarette-stuffed-up-the-butt-cheek jokes, and full rectal mooning, interspersed with a score that would make the Four Seasons sound like Metallica, *Grease* kept the audience—filled with soccer moms and their vile suburban progeny—in absolute stitches. As was the case with so many other shows that I saw during that false spring, the production had the smell of death about it, with the actress playing Rizzo serving her second tour of duty in the show and looking like she was definitely walking her last mile.

Broadway performers, along with many musicians, artists, comedians, and even journalists, belong to a large class best described as the *working famous*: people who have a certain public profile, have notched a few points on the scoreboard, and who may even have appeared on "Late Night with Conan O'Brien," but who still have to hustle for every buck they earn. The day I turned up, some of the cast members of *Grease* had that thousand-mile stare. Iowa, it should be noted, is about a thousand miles from New York.

In Tom Clancy's otherwise unreadable *Op-Center: Acts of War,* there is an illuminating passage where one of the characters explains how to survive physical torture after falling into the hands of the enemy.

"The key was not to be tense," Clancy writes. "Tension only tightened the flesh, stretching the skin cells and exacerbating the pain. Tension also focused the mind on the pain. Victims were told to try to count to themselves, to divide the suffering into manageable segments of three or five seconds. They had to think of making it to the next plateau rather than to the end."

Frankly, I think Clancy's completely full of shit. I tried as hard as humanly possible to apply his elaborate antitorture technique while watching *Grease,* and it simply didn't work. First, I told myself to concentrate on making it through the first act. Impossible. Then I said to myself, "If you can just manage to sit through 'Freddy, My Love' you can survive this ordeal." No dice. Finally, I broke "Look at Me, I'm Sandra Dee" down into tiny segments—not a chorus, not a verse, not a whole bar, but a series of single notes—hoping to survive until the next note. A complete and utter failure. Maybe Tom Clancy's strategy will work if you've been crucified by members of Saddam Hussein's Republican Guards and are having fire ants forced up your rectum while your genitals are being blowtorched, but it won't work with *Grease.*

I remember reading that one of the sadistic techniques the feds used during the Siege of Waco was to force David Koresh's followers to listen to abominable music played at ear-shattering volumes at all hours of the day and night, in order to drive them more insane than they already were.

I am positive that Janet Reno owns the soundtrack to *Grease*.

Needless to say, *Victor/Victoria* occupied a prominent position on my road to Golgotha. I had seen the movie when it came out in 1982, hated every minute of it, and saw no reason to believe that a live version of the show would be any better now that an even more mummified Julie Andrews was cast in the role. I am also no big fan of director Blake Edwards, a putative genius whose relentless decline began as soon as he stopped working with Peter Sellers, an authentic genius. All in all, the show promised to be a nightmare.

Ah, promises, promises. *Victor/Victoria* was an absurdly dated piece of work, a frothy cross-dresser's romp that did not resonate with much vigor in the age of Dennis Rodman. It had no good songs, no memorable dance routines, and its message was infantile. Everything in *Victor/Victoria* was straight off-the-shelf. For a fleeting moment, this gave me a newfound, perverse, probably unhealthy respect for the work of Andrew Lloyd Webber, because, with the single exception of *Sunset Boulevard*, his scores were so bad that you could at least remember the songs you hated.

The difference between an *Evita*, a *Cats*, or a *Phantom* and a *Victor/Victoria* was much akin to the difference between bands that sucked like Bread and Chicago and bands that sucked like Toto and Rush. You could remember why you hated Bread and Chicago because songs like "Baby, I'm-A Want You" and "Color My World" were burned into your consciousness with a red-hot branding iron dipped in a cauldron of molten hooey. But Toto you merely remembered as a band that sucked.

Rush, I don't even remember.

The weak score notwithstanding, Julie Andrews's *Victor/ Victoria* was not the cornucopia of imbecility I had expected, and even hoped, it would be. Though no spring chicken and thus much too old for the role, Andrews was perfectly serviceable in her schoolmarmish, music-hallish sort of way; Tony Roberts was excellent; and Rachel York, playing a ditzy moll, was hilarious. I also liked the sets, the supporting cast, and the clever way the show was staged. Though it pains me to admit it, the musical, with Julie Andrews at the helm, was relatively painless.

Liza Minnelli's *Victor/Victoria* was a whole other story. Liza had been recruited for the role because *Victor/Victoria* is a star-driven monolith, and Liza is the ultimate star, at least by Broadway's substandard standards. Alas, Liza has never been much of an actress, was a bit out of shape at the time, and was already far too androgynous to be credible in the lead role. Asking Liza Minnelli to masquerade as a man was like asking Michael Jackson to masquerade as a man. It confused an already confused issue.

There was also something about the audience that made me feel kind of queasy. The Liza crowd forms one of those bizarre nexuses in American culture where gay men intersect with middle-American heterosexual tourists, Liza having inherited the demographic group that was once shared by Liberace and Ethel Merman. There was something unsettling about sitting in a room where one-third of the crowd consisted of men wearing House of Gilligan leisure wear, one-third was made up of women dressed like Fran Drescher, and one-third was comprised of men in neatly pressed Dockers with perfect little sweaters. It was like wandering into a room filled with a thousand pastry chefs and five hundred big-game hunters. How did these people find each other? At what psychic level did they connect with one another? Did they all go back to the Howard Johnson's after the show to drink boilermakers and watch Joan Crawford movies? And why was I here?

Liza's *Victor/Victoria* was one of the many events on which my thirteen-year-old daughter Bridget agreed to tag along. Later in my adventures, when I had exhausted the more conventional popular diversions and was spending most of my time at medieval tournaments in rural New York, she would express dismay at my unwholesome entertainment industry overtures. But *Victor/Victoria* was right up her alley. *She* wanted to see it because she likes Broadway shows, no matter how bad they are. And *I* was interested in having her see it because I wanted to gauge her reaction to the Minnelli Enigma.

Why? Because a phenomenon that has always fascinated me is that category of things that suck so bad even your kids know they suck. Here I am talking about things kids can independently decipher as appalling without any cultural conditioning from their parents. For example, my daughter did not arrive at the indisputable conclusion that soccer eats it raw until she had played forty-two 1–0 games over a five-year period and finally recognized that there was no light at the end of that particular tunnel. Similarly, kids do not know instinctively that they should never accept candy, doughnuts, or rides from guys who hang around diners in threadbare POW-MIA jackets thumbing through well-worn copies of the Warren Commission report. These things, sad to say, have to be learned.

But other things kids can figure out without any outside assistance. Children do not need to be told that free summer concerts featuring Johnny Maestro and the Brooklyn Bridge singing "The Worst That Could Happen" are vastly over-priced. Kids do not need to be told that virtually anything ending in the word *Collins*—Phil, Joan, Jackie, Tom—is satanic; it's in their DNA coding. Kids *do* need to be taught that Red Lobster sucks, but they can figure out that Taco Bell sucks all by themselves. For example, when I splurged on a trip to Taco Bell the night before the 1997 Super Bowl, my son noticed that while everyone else in the country had ditched their Cowboys and 49ers outerwear in favor of spanking-new, front-runner supreme Green Bay Packers regalia and those foolish plastic cheeseheads, the patrons at Taco Bell were wearing chintzy, Made-in-Honduras New England Patriots jackets. Amateur losers themselves, they instinctively gravitated toward the official garb of professional losers.

This being the case, I was fascinated to find out what Bridget made of Liza Minnelli's performance in *Victor/Victoria*. Right off the bat, she noticed that the audience was kind of, well, eclectic. She also realized that the story was kind of, well, weird. And when the audience rose as one to applaud Liza's grand entrance, she knew that something unusual was going on. The audience had not risen as one when John Cullum made his grand entrance in *Show Boat*. Nor had the audience risen as one when we saw Lou Diamond Phillips take the stage in *The King and I*. Lou doesn't have that kind of following.

We suffered through the show as best we could. Liza was stiff, poorly prepared, a corpse of a hoofer, out of sync with the cast, allegedly feuding with the absent, bedridden Tony Roberts. I said nothing about this to Bridget at any point during the performance. I didn't want to tip my hand. Only when

Liza's final thunderous curtain call had died down and we headed for the exit did I ask her what she thought of the play.

"Well, it's not like *Guys and Dolls* or *Crazy for You*," she judiciously observed. "It doesn't have any great songs."

I agreed. Then I asked what she thought of the whole Liza situation.

She shrugged.

"She's Judy Garland's daughter, right?" she asked.

I nodded.

"I guess that explains it," she answered.

At this juncture, I should point out that shows were by no means isolated, miserable events in otherwise ordinary days. On the contrary (or, as Joan Collins would say, "au contraire"), I would often set up a full schedule of atrocities to maximize my exposure to the transparently horrific. For example, the day I saw *Grease* I started off by reading my pitiful local newspaper—Gannett, of course—while sampling the legendary vile coffee and crullers purveyed by Dunkin' Donuts. Then I read a few chapters of *The Thorn Birds*. Lunchtime found me dining at T.G.I.F.'s, where I struggled, with no great success, to force down the monstrous cheddar cheese and broccoli soup, while off in the distance Elton John blared "I'm Still Standing." Which is more than you can say for anyone who tried eating the cheddar cheese and broccoli soup.

As Guns N' Roses nuked their way through the loudspeakers at ear-piercing levels, my waitdude vainly attempted to recite the house specials. For once in my life, I was happy to be in a restaurant where Axl Rose was shrieking at ear-piercing levels. There are some things in life that you're better off not hearing, and the T.G.I.F. list of house specials is one of them. I have the same feeling about the sexual techniques practiced at bars named *Le Petit Souris Mignon* in downtown Tangiers: I don't want to know.

After lunch at T.G.I.F.'s, I took in *Grease* before repairing to the Times Square branch of the Olive Garden, on the prowl for some well-earned *capellini pomodoro* or *ravioli della casa*. The Olive Garden had long fascinated me because it exuded a kind of Red Lobster snootiness; although its spectacular array of *pasta e fagioli* and *penne fra diavolo* was just a cut above *tortellini da Chef Boyardee,* both the clientele and the waitstaff clearly deemed themselves immeasurably more upscale than the peons dining at the local Roy Rogers. This illusion was supported not only by the liberal use of such bizarre Italo-Inglese neologisms as *Brownie Decadenza* and *Cheesecake Ghirardelli* but by the luxurious pseudo-Vesuvian decor with its spreading palm trees and sepia-toned photographs of humble Neapolitan peasants cavorting near the Leaning Tower of Pisa. Sadly, this was an illusion that was brutally shattered by the preeminence of New Jersey Devils dining garb and by the huge winking eye positioned on the wall directly across the street, which read:

PEEP

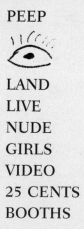

LAND
LIVE
NUDE
GIRLS
VIDEO
25 CENTS
BOOTHS

The illusion of class was also subverted by certain unfortunate deviations from the normal standards of fine cuisine for which the Olive Garden has long been revered. When I first inspected the menu, I was dazzled by the Olive Garden's alchemical use of the English language, predicated on the theory that if you used lots of colorful wording to describe your grim fare, it could magically transform a repellent morass of what appeared to be congealed mucus into a truly wondrous *zuppa toscana*.

But as we all know, even alchemy has its limits. The bowl of soup I received was repugnant to at least two senses—both the eyes and the taste buds—it having no discernible smell. A fearsome quagmire of deeply failed vegetal and lactic ingredients, the *zuppa toscana* was so awful that not only was I unable to eat it, I was unable to look at it. Gathering a couple of napkins together, I quickly interred the offensive item in an impromptu shroud, a makeshift burial for a leprous warrior slain in an unnecessary, easily preventable war.

For the first time since I had embarked on my epic adventure, I had found a restaurant capable of competing with Red Lobster on its own terms. Overpriced. Quixotically snooty. Preposterous.

Loathsome.

Throughout the winter, spring, and early summer of 1997, I dined in many other dreadful New York eateries. But none could match the Olive Garden for sheer chutzpah in support of a profoundly troubled menu. As for theatrical fare, I spent many long afternoons in pursuit of a play that could mount even slight competition to *Cats* and *Grease* for intellectual vacuity. *Victor/Victoria* was bad, but not bad enough. *Miss Saigon, Les Miserables,* and *Phantom of the Opera* were all horrendous in their own little ways, but ultimately their awfulness was of Lilliputian dimensions by comparison with the aforementioned fiascoes. In the end, only one play could hold a candle to *Cats* and *Grease* for pure fatuity. That play was *Jekyll and Hyde.*

Jekyll and Hyde, which opened in April 1997, had an interesting pedigree. Unlike most bad musicals, which start out on Broadway and then drag their carcasses off to sepulchral little supper club theaters all across the land, *Jekyll and Hyde* had been playing for years out in the hinterland and had only now made it to the Great White Way. As such, it seemed antiquated even before it opened. The music, cast very much in the Lloyd Webberian mold, was hypnotically puerile, with verses like:

> *"He'll kill us if we let him.*
> *They'd better go and get him."*

Worse still, the sappy, syrupy numbers that dominated the show seemed entirely inappropriate for what was, after all, one of the greatest horror stories of all time. Any minute, you expected the doomed heroine to start singing:

> *"Tomorrow, tomorrow,*
> *He'll flay me tomorrow.*
> *It's only a day away."*

But what truly rendered the musical intoxicatingly moronic was the ridiculous casting of the lead role and the absurd stage business utilized to effect the effete Henry Jekyll's transformations into the atavistic Edward Hyde. The day I stopped by, the male lead was being played by the matinee understudy, a portly, weak-chinned, ponytailed fussbudget who bore an uncanny resemblance to Tony Little, the overbearing blond-haired fitness guru who is always turning up in late-night infomercials, looking for all the world like the Venice Beach reincarnation of Thor.

Whenever the script called for Henry Jekyll to turn into Edward Hyde, the actor simply loosened his ponytail, shook his impressive mane, and tried to look scary. Here the director of this benighted musical had gotten things completely ass-backwards.

To my knowledge, medical doctors didn't wear ponytails back in Victorian times: It would make them look too much like an L.A. waiter, circa 1989, brandishing the Key lime pie. But viewed from the perspective of the contemporary theatergoer, namely me, the presence of the ponytail had even more sinister cultural ramifications. Young men with long hair are generally viewed as cool—Brad Pitt, Keanu Reeves, and yes, even Lou Diamond Phillips. But young men with ponytails are considered just plain revolting, because the ponytail is the calling card of only two types of people:

1. the yuppie lawyer who defends people named Bruno the Chicken-Man by day while listening to Jethro Tull at night;

2. that L.A. waiter we previously discussed.

The effect of this miscue was to discombobulate the intelligent theatergoer. That is, me. Henry Jekyll, as defined by our Anglo-American lore, is supposed to be a gallant but doomed scientist who brings about his demise by daring to venture into a domain where man was never meant to go. Edward Hyde is supposed to be the second coming of Moloch. But because the producers of this play had given Henry Jekyll an entirely foolish ponytail, he came off as a big galoot right from the start, whereas Edward Hyde seemed to possess a kind of impish Steven Tyler pizzazz. Frankly, I could never decide who to root for in this duel of the testosteronally tressed titans.

And yet it was while I was watching this wee, undernourished excuse for a play that I had an astonishing revelation of my own. Like Henry Jekyll, I had launched my experiment for purely scientific reasons: to find out how the culturally starved lived and to learn what eating too much *zuppa toscana* after seeing Kenny G would do to my digestive system. Like Henry Jekyll, I was initially repelled by society's lower depths but had gradually found the lure of the underworld oddly enticing. And like Henry Jekyll, I was finding it more and more difficult to control my struggle between the diametrically opposed forces that were engaged in a battle royal for my very soul.

I had pinpointed this dilemma a mere two hours earlier as I took my seat in the last row, next to a charming, well-dressed, middle-aged woman sporting a world-weary look.

"Have you heard anything good about this play?" she asked me.

"No," I replied. "Everything I've heard about it leads me to believe that it's absolutely putrid."

She giggled.

"Then why are you here?" she inquired.

"I'm writing a book about how awful things can be," I explained. "Why are you here?"

"I've seen everything else on Broadway," she replied.

We chatted some more, and then the lights dimmed. Almost immediately, the woman started shaking her head in disbelief.

"This is horrible," she murmured, as the nightmare unfolded in front of our very eyes.

"Shhh," I hushed her, tartly. "I don't want to miss a word of it."

Touched by a Devil

On June 11, 1997, I had an experience that was to change my life forever. That was the day I had direct physical contact with Geraldo Rivera.

I had not intended for things to turn out this way, but they did. Having sent away for tickets to the Prince of Evil's daytime TV show several weeks earlier, I reported to the ice-cold West 57th Street studio where the program is taped, intending to sit in the audience and write my weekly *TV Guide* column about what I saw and heard and felt and re-gurgitated.

I did not expect the experience to be pleasant, and it was not. The subject of the show was "Baby-Faced Killers," with Geraldo weaving one of his usual incoherent pastiches, link-ing the two kids who murdered a wino in Central Park with the two guys who lured a pair of pizza delivery men to their deaths in rural New Jersey with the Jersey girl who deposited her newly born baby in a trash can at her junior prom. Ger-aldo, with his finely honed ability to separate the grist from the mill, the wheat from the chaff, the ying from the yang, could detect a disturbing pattern here. These youthful killers were young, restless, and out for blood.

It spoke volumes about our society.

At this juncture in his career, Geraldo was desperately trying to reinvent himself as a professional journalist, and not some Rainbow Coalition doofus who had once taken skin grafts from his buttocks in order to surgically repair his face. It was a daring undertaking, not unlike Pol Pot trying to redeem himself in the eyes of his countrymen. ("I admit that I made some mistakes in the past; that whole Killing Fields interlude is a deep personal embarrassment. But I think I have learned from the indiscretions of my youth, and I truly believe that it is now time to go forward.")

One gambit Geraldo had devised to make himself seem more like Tom Brokaw or Edward R. Murrow was to book "experts" who looked as if they'd completed a few years of college. Geraldo's guests that day included a whole galaxy of such talk show Erasmuses, most prominently an expert on child rearing who felt that the best way to prevent one's children from growing up to be child murderers was to give them a good whack upside the head from time to time. Fittingly, the man's head looked as if it had been subjected to a fair amount of formative cranial pummeling.

Geraldo was in fine form that afternoon, mechanically expressing shock and outrage at all these horrible crimes whenever the camera was on him, then wading into the audience to press the flesh as soon as the director cut away for a commercial. As for the audience, it was the usual assortment of simpletons, nitwits, and ne'er-do-wells, intermingled with some brain-dead college students and a handful of befuddled tourists who looked like they'd wandered into the wrong grog house and been forcibly gang-pressed into Geraldo's Royal Navy. Plus, of course, me.

The whole thing was quite disgusting, what with Geraldo's hammy consoling of a woman whose child had been murdered, followed by some cheerful chatting with audience members, and his sublimely idiotic interview of the entire family of one of the slain pizza men, followed by more genial schmoozing. As Mom, Dad, Sis, and Fiancée Pizza Guy trooped onto the stage, I wondered if Geraldo had actually paid them to come onto his show and make a public spectacle of their grief. Didn't anyone in this country mourn their dead children in private anymore? Or was it a cultural axiom that a soul could not go to its eternal reward until it had been immortalized on "Geraldo" or "Jerry Springer," that it would wander around the universe forever, a disembodied spirit without a final resting place, until Geraldo told its parents: "We all feel for you." Or was this one of those social aberrations the rest of us couldn't understand because it was a *Jersey thang*?

Sitting in that arctic studio with fifty to sixty knuckleheads was not an enjoyable way to spend the afternoon. Nevertheless, it was an experience I could have survived. But then something totally unexpected occurred. As I sat in my chair during a commercial, fiddling with my notes, I saw a dark shadow looming up in front of me. To my horror, there stood Geraldo, proffering his hand in friendship. Being a courteous sort, I clasped it, gazing up into his hideous, smiling face. No sooner had our palms locked than I felt an electric jolt race through my nervous system. Right then and there, I could feel the dark power of Satan coursing through my veins.

It was the end of the world as I knew it.

From the moment I shook hands with Geraldo Rivera, a dramatic shift occurred in my personality. Suddenly I found myself rushing home in the middle of the day to watch anything having to do with the World Wrestling Federation. In-explicably, I was glued to MTV's "KISS Unplugged," finding it so enthralling that I taped my own copy for my multiple viewing pleasure. I begged off a dinner date to finish Clive Cussler's interminable *Raise the Titanic!* ("Pitt stood frozen in time, like some unspeakable apparition that had risen from the depths of a watery hell.") I got into NASCAR big time. And even when I did take a respite from this noxious fare later in the week and attended a concert by Gil Shaham and the Orchestra of St. Luke's, I found myself languishing through Beethoven's Violin Concerto, then thundering off at intermission to phone my kids and make sure they were tap-ing that special two-hour episode of "Walker, Texas Ranger."

Of course, I knew why I was behaving so oddly. I had started out like Henry Jekyll, a student of the human con-dition who had embarked on a bold experiment to under-stand how the criminal mind operates. In order to do this, I had occasionally slipped into the role of Edward Hyde, the depraved brute. Now, after shaking hands with Geraldo Ri-vera, I could no longer predict when these sudden transfor-mations would occur, nor could I control their ultimate direction. Like the well-meaning but morally flawed Jekyll, I was slowly succumbing to the far greater power of Hyde. I was being sucked into the darkness.

Little by little, my kids started to notice that something terrible had befallen their father. My daughter thought it odd that I should ask her to accompany me to New York City on the hottest day of the year to attend a matinee of the long-running off-Broadway hit *Tony and Tina's Wedding*. The play is one of those gala participatory affairs where the audience attends a bogus Italian wedding in a Greenwich Village church, then troops around the corner and up the block for a reception in a mob-style lounge. It was the sort of moronic clattertrap I had long despised, as evidenced by the fact that I once pulled a Swiss army knife on a greaser actor at a Murder Mystery fund-raiser and told him I would cut out his tongue if he ever again dared to ask me, "What's up, daddyo?"

Why then did I find myself embracing Tina herself as we emerged into the sweltering heat outside St. John's Church? Why was I high-fiving the various Dominics, Nunzios, and Vinnies who made up the wedding party? And why, when the bride's gay brother formed a conga line at the reception hall, was I thrusting out my hands in frantic V-shaped gestures and bellowing "Evita! Evita! Evita!" at the top of my lungs?

By the time the moment had come at Vinnie Black's Coliseum to toast the newlyweds with the dirt-cheap champagne supplied by the theater producers, my daughter realized that several gears in my personality had slipped. As the fake Irish priest who had performed the wedding clasped my shoulders and asked, "Is everything all right, my son?" she finally turned to me and said, "I think we get the idea, Dad. Can we go?"

But I didn't want to go. I was having the time of my life. Staring across the table, I spied a pair of geriatric curmudgeons who had clearly been roped into attending a play they were not enjoying. In their bewildered facial expressions I could see a perfect reflection of the snooty, elitist, overly judgmental prig I had been before my fatal handshake with Geraldo Rivera released me just a few weeks earlier. And believe you me, I didn't like what I saw.

"Lighten up, you old farts!" I bellowed across the table at the stunned old geezers. "Get out on the dance floor and boogie like the rest of us."

Eventually, my daughter, feigning a coma, managed to drag me away from the spellbindingly hokey event. But my appetite for the vulgar, the obvious, the cornballish had not yet been sated. Insisting that I was dying of thirst, I forced the exhausted thirteen-year-old to accompany me to the Greenwich Village branch of the Jekyll and Hyde Restaurant, where I gorged myself on a fiendishly overpriced, preternaturally bland Frankenstein Burger. Then it was off to see *Speed II*, which we already knew was a bomb, even though she would have preferred to see *Con Air*. By the end of the day, as I sat down to read a few pages of *Dune,* the evidence was incontrovertible: The demons of suck had sunk their fangs deep into my throat and I was powerless to remove them.

Yes, the cancer was spreading. One summer afternoon, coming home from the city, I picked up a copy of *Men Are from Mars, Women Are from Venus. Men Are from Mars* is John Gray's enormously popular, 286-page book, which explains that men and women are very different and have a difficult time communicating with one another. I had long believed that Mr. Gray was on to something here. On the train, a pug-faced woman engaged me in conversation about the book, observing that it was the sort of literary phenomenon that occurred but once in a generation, following in the rich tradition of *I'm OK, You're OK* or *The Thorn Birds.* A few weeks earlier, I would have pole-axed this gorgon, but now I sat there unfazed by her chatter. Then I went home and read *I'm OK, You're OK.* I was losing control fast.

The situation steadily deteriorated. One sleepless July

night I went downstairs and cued up Liberace's mawkish version of "I'll Be Seeing You" on the compact-disc player. This is a song on which Liberace not only sings but talks. I had long believed that the only singer in the history of American music who could get away with talking in the middle of a song was Elvis. Indeed, Elvis's ability to talk in the middle of "Are You Lonesome Tonight?" without being lynched was the clearest sign of the cultural hegemony he exercised over a macho nation that usually didn't put up with that kind of crap. Yet tonight, I found myself oddly diverted and charmed by Liberace's arrant patter. This was a very disturbing development indeed.

The same night I listened to *Liberace's Greatest Hits*, I started reading W. E. B. Griffin's festively stupid *Honor Bound*, a ludicrous yarn about Nazi spies in Argentina during the Second World War. The premise of the book is that the United States needs to blow up a German submarine, but has to do it covertly, because otherwise "there would be an inevitable public outcry—fueled by the Germans—against American violation of Argentinian neutrality." Ordinarily, a plot line as idiotic as this would have caused me to toss the book into the fireplace. But no, there I was, well past midnight, eyes riveted to words like:

" 'Colonel Peron, may I present Brigadeführer von Niebermann, Oberst Susser, and Hauptmann Freiherr von Wachstein?' von Ruppersdorf said."

"Fine with me," I thought. "And bring over Übermensch Friedrich Krueger and Messerschmitt Überkamplieder Andreas Wollenweider while you're at it."

Mind you, there were still moments of lucidity when I recognized the depths to which I had plunged. For example,

I knew that Jimmy Carter's latest book *Living Faith* was going to be ghastly. This was a knockoff job in which Carter explained how God had helped him through the tough patches in his career. Needless to say, Carter was not especially lucid on the subject of why God allowed Ronald Reagan to kick his ass in 1980.

As I read this book, I realized that Jimmy Carter and I worshiped a very different God. Carter's God watches over a man who writes poetry like this to his wife:

> *She'd smile, and birds would feel that they no longer*
> *had to sing, or it may be I failed*
> *to hear their song.*

My God hates double-digit prime interest rates, and will move heaven and earth to make sure a ninny like Carter is quickly ejected from the White House.

And yet, knowing all this, I read the book from cover to cover.

I had a fruitful outing when I attended *Victor/Victoria* for the third time, this time with Raquel Welch in the starring role. It was an experience totally different from the evenings I saw Julie Andrews and Liza Minnelli in the same role. For one, the audience was composed almost entirely of tourists, and was thus overwhelmingly heterosexual. Two, as was the case with Elaine Page's *Sunset Boulevard*, the show had the smell of death about it, with plenty of empty seats in the back. Three, the show was even more confusing than the first two times I saw it.

Of the three stars, Welch was the most overtly feminine, the one least likely to pull off the transformation from Victoria to Victor. Even when she switched to male evening dress, with her hair pulled back, she still looked like a woman. Well, like Leona Helmsley. Surprisingly short, alarmingly top-heavy, disconcertingly plump, she didn't look like the kind of man any Chicago gangster worth his salt would fall for. She looked like a woman.

Welch was terrible in the part, worse than Liza. She couldn't sing, wasn't much of a dancer, and, like Minnelli, seemed to devote most of her energy to not tripping. When she executed a scissors kick during the big jazz number at the end of Act I, I realized why this show in all of its manifestations had always made me feel uncomfortable. Julie Andrews is a puffy matron. Liza is a paunchy fifty-something. Raquel is a chunky fifty-seven-year-old. Watching these postmenopausal show-offs executing kicks designed for Bebe Neuwirth or Charlotte D'Amboise made my stomach turn. It was like watching your mom vamping it up on top of the piano. All right, let's lay our cards right on the table: It was gross.

There was one other vital element that separated this performance from the two previous ones. When I went to see Julie Andrews early in the year, the audience rose as one when she first appeared on the stage and rose as one when she descended to the footlights at the end. When I went to see Liza Minnelli a couple of months later, the audience rose as one when she first appeared on the stage and rose as one when she approached the footlights at the end. When I went to see Raquel Welch, the audience sat as one when she first appeared on the stage, and sat as one when she came down to the footlights at the end. Only one person rose from his seat to applaud her.

Me.

That's when I knew that this thing was getting out of hand.

★　　★　　★

Yet, inexorably, my decline continued. I spent an entire evening prowling New York comedy clubs, frantically seeking a female comedian willing to talk about something other than her vagina, and a male comic willing to talk about something other than, well, vaginas. I became intoxicated by the grotesque parody of cappuccino that they dare to serve in the Astor Place Kmart. Like everything else in this culturally incongruous merchandising emporium, which sits in the heart of the East Village like a Tupac Shakur impersonator at a Shriners convention, the coffee seemed to be made of polyester. Yet every time I wandered into that neighborhood, I caught myself involuntarily drifting up to the second floor for a double jolt of café manqué.

The movies on my current rental list were uniformly horrendous. In fact, they were so bad they had not even made my earlier list of movies too bad to watch. *Boxing Helena*, in which a woman is victimized by a surgical stalker's unconventional medical techniques and discovers too late that none of the procedures are covered by her HMO because she failed to get a referral. *Leprechaun*, a ferociously Hibernophobic horror flick with a suspiciously large number of English-sounding names in the credits. *Bordello of Blood*, which was just what it sounds like. *Cabin Boy*, which was even worse than just what it sounds like. *Car Wash. Caligula.* Oh, what gems they were! Take *Live Nude Girls*. During a hen party attended by four old friends, Dana Delany reveals her innermost secret: that she has always wanted to be publicly spanked on her bare bottom by an aging gangster who inserts his cigar in her garter belt, though, sadly, nowhere else, while punishing her. Boy, if they'd used more of this kind of footage on "China Beach," that show would have run as long as "Gunsmoke."

Another disturbing side effect of my illness was that I

was starting to let my experiment affect my work. In my *TV Guide* column I raved about "Xena: Warrior Princess" and "Charles Grodin." I said nice things about Larry King. I blew a big kiss to the Home Shopping Network. I sent a valentine to Bob Barker at "The Price Is Right."

Sure, every once in a while I snapped out of it and reverted to my Henry Jekyll personality, raking Arsenio Hall over the coals and ripping the shit out of a major TV network's plans to give Sarah Ferguson her own TV show. But then, as a form of penance, I went out and rented *Coming to America,* and reread the part in Ferguson's autobiography where she says: "I have always sailed close to the wind, through storm and calm, and over the roughest whitecaps."

I even suggested to my wife that we get these words embroidered on a pillow cover and send it to my mom. She did not think this was a very good idea.

Inevitably, my descent into the maelstrom began to take a toll on my family. My kids wondered why we were spending so many summer evenings at Taco Bell eating precisely the kinds of meals whose global exportation Emiliano Zapata and Pancho Villa had died to prevent. They were even more perplexed when we would stop off for profoundly unsatisfactory ice cream at Carvel's, rather than the usual Häagen-Dazs, and then go home to watch reruns of "Baywatch," which even they, with their callow, unformed minds, recognized as moronic. They were baffled by the amount of time I spent in Wal-Marts looking for rare Reba McEntire CDs, or on AOL downloading photos of the Judds. They were hopelessly confused when I sat in the family room watching ancient tapes of Liz Taylor tributes and Diane Sawyer interviewing the Duchess of Pork. Kids, it should be pointed out, are not sophisticated enough to tell which of the two is the more satanic. Of course, neither am I.

It was not until things turned hopelessly medieval, however, that my family realized how dire the situation had become. One glorious Sunday afternoon I badgered my wife and children into accompanying me to the Renaissance Faire held in Sterling Forest, about twenty miles west of my home and forty miles north of New York City. This was one of those places where you had to fork over an enormous amount of your hard-earned cash to get in and then they didn't give you anything in return. So, in that sense, it was very much like the Middle Ages. For hours and hours, I walked around what was basically a Dark Ages mall, filled with shops selling jewelry, herbs, and other rubbish of ersatz Carolingian provenance while strolling minstrels in leotards and doublets who looked like unemployed American studies professors from Montclair Community College sang blithely nauseating airs about courtly love. The food was pseudo-Saxon, the beverages bogus-Beowulfian, the entertainment faux-feudal. Scant months ago, I would have stood there glowering, wishing the Black Death would make a surprise visit and clean out the entire park. But now my attitude was: *Honi soit qui mal y pense* (Different strokes for different folks).

Medievalry seemed to be a big hit with the local white trash, an army of born serfs who had magically deluded themselves into thinking that they had been lords of the manor in another time and place. The Faire was literally bursting at the seams with stout yeomen, hale-fellows-well-met, and wenches who were not nearly as comely as they thought they were, but who still thought they had an outside shot at bedding the falconer. Some were in the employ of the theme park itself, and some merely turned up in period costume each Saturday and Sunday because getting dressed up as a Knight of the Round Table who had plighted his troth to find the Holy Grail made a nice change from wearing that Wendy's uniform. Most of the impersonators tried to stay in character and got miffed if you asked: "Good morrow, sir, knowest thou the Mets-Cubs score?" No, even they were not entirely impervious to irony.

The tournament that was the showpiece of the Faire was engagingly stupid. Poncy guys with huge mustaches tried to act like Merovingian studs on furlough from the Crusades, but it was impossible to believe that any of these whoresons could have ever skewered a Saracen dog. One joker kept missing the cabbages he was supposed to be decapitating with his lance, and another clown attacked the targets with his horse cantering at about two miles an hour. The crowd booed, recognizing that this was not the way Holy Jerusalem had been wrested from the iron grip of the heathen Turk. On the other hand, we *were* in that bizarre section of rural New York that forms a kind of Parallel New Jersey, so you had to make allowances.

My son, aged ten, found the whole premise of the Renaissance Faire profoundly idiotic. He pointed out that some of the people were walking around in Arthurian costumes dating from the misty days of yore (he did not actually use the phrase "misty days of yore"), some were dressed in armor dating from the era of the Crusades, and some were decked out like the Three Musketeers, who lived hundreds of years after the Dark Ages ended. He knew this for a fact, because he had seen the movie with Charlie Sheen.

"Nobody likes a purist," I snapped at him, miffed that he was ruining my afternoon. "Now get thee hence and fetch me a flagon of mead."

French Leave

Although the Renaissance Faire chomped the royal prong, my family had to literally drag me away kicking and screaming from the sham liege lords, vassals, tinkers, and costermongers who had become my sworn kinsmen. It was now apparent that the situation warranted desperate measures. It was vital that I have a change of scenery, that I remove myself from the line of fire until a path out of this madness presented itself. And so, I decided to leave the country, theorizing that if I completely isolated myself from low-brow American culture, my illness might pass.

For a number of reasons, France seemed like the ideal destination. For starters, the French hate Americans, and because of the language barrier their civilization is largely estranged from our own. Nobody in France knows who John Tesh is. Nobody in France knows who Pat Robertson is. The French neither know nor care about Robert Fulghum. Most important, there is no such thing as a French rock 'n' roll fantasy camp where for $2,795—plus airfare—you get to spend a long weekend with the lead guitarist from Foreigner.

It also helped that my sister- and brother-in-law lived in a tiny village in an isolated region of southern France where nobody was ever likely to mention Richard Bey or tell me how much they enjoyed that last Travis Tritt CD. Nor did I fear that by fleeing to France I would merely replace my addiction to American suckiness with a new addiction to Gallic suckiness. Cultural suck is bred in the bone, making it impossible for a single human being to consistently feel his skin crawl in a foreign language. Though the French count among their citizens people who are every bit as hooty as Billy Joel and Tony Danza, I had not spent my entire life consciously avoiding them, so succumbing to the siren song of their suckiness would carry no psychic resonance. Actually, the French, for all their faults (Jerry Lewis, Mickey Rourke, Pétain), do not have any natives as bad as Billy Joel, but they do occasionally get in the ballpark.

My preparations for the voyage indicate how little confidence I had that my trip was going to be a success. Though I had assured my family that I would go cold turkey and immediately estrange myself from all the cultural icons oppressing me, my promise was not sincere. After my family had gone to bed on the night of July 22, I stole downstairs and quietly repacked my bag. Out came the Tom McGuane and Iris Murdoch novels I had vowed to read during my vacation, and in went *The Winds of War*, *Rich Man, Poor Man*, and *Jonathan Livingston Seagull*. The fifteen Elvis Costello, Graham Parker, Freedy Johnston, Warren Zevon, and Richard Thompson records I had promised to take on the trip were now surreptitiously replaced by Kenny G, John Tesh, Abba, Genesis, Billy Joel, Phil Collins, Enya, and Liberace. All those back issues of *The Atlantic* and *Harper's* that I'd been stockpiling were replaced by spanking-new copies of *Musclemag International*, *Soap Opera Digest*, *Metal Edge*,

Tattoo, and *Richard Petty's Stockcar*. I had not entirely conceded that this trip was doomed to failure. But I didn't want to wind up in the psychiatric wing of some lugubrious French hospital after going into seizures because I couldn't get my daily fix of "Captain Jack" or Jack Canfield's *Chicken Soup for the Soul*.

When I alighted at Charles de Gaulle Airport later that day, I was in for a huge surprise. From the moment I set foot in France, I felt like a new man. The very first night I arrived in Amiens, an hour north of Paris, I started reading a book by André Gide and watched a Belgian movie called *C'est Arrivé Près de Chez Vous*. The low-budget, black-and-white movie dealt with a serial killer who hires a camera team to follow him around while he murders innocent people. In one memorable sequence, the killer stumbles upon another serial killer who also has a camera team following him around filming his crimes. Not surprisingly, he kills him.

Twenty-four hours earlier, I would have found this kind of pretentious European nonsense completely unwatchable and would have been prowling the streets for a Pauly Shore film. But now that I had removed myself from a milieu that was slowly asphyxiating me, I found the film quite thought-provoking, clever, and entertaining. Perhaps my ploy was working.

The next day was equally encouraging. I spent the morning finishing the book by Gide, then passed the afternoon looking at paintings by Courbet and Boucher at the Musee de Picardie in Amiens. Two days earlier, you couldn't have gotten me to look at a painting unless it was signed by Leroy Niemann or Tony Curtis, but now I found myself reverting to my old snooty, pre-Geraldo self. Later in the day, I listened to some gorgeous cello music by the vastly underrated Gabriel Fauré and closed out the day by watching another artsy, pretentious French film. Though I tried not to feel overly enthusiastic about what was taking place, the events of the last thirty-six hours allowed me the hope that even if my disease had not been completely cured, it had at least gone into remission.

Late in the afternoon, I visited Amiens's magnificent cathedral with a French friend who had once worked as a tour guide in the building. After we gazed up at the glorious stained-glass windows and the exquisite statuary, she led me inside the sanctuary and showed me the ornate carvings on the chairs where the choir customarily sat. At the bottom of one seat was a carving of a dinner scene. My friend told me to stick my hand underneath and feel the hidden surface. Incredibly, the craftsmen who had designed this furniture had actually carved the feet of the festive celebrants under the chairs, even though no one would ever see their loving artistry. They did it for the greater glory of God, because they wanted to get things exactly right. They wanted to make sure that their work was absolutely flawless.

This briefly reminded me of the decision by the producers of *Cannonball Run II* to include a cameo appearance by Don Knotts in a film that already showcased Dom DeLuise, Ricardo Montalban, and Jamie Farr, but I quickly realized that this was an inappropriate analogy, and let it go.

The next two weeks were an absolute paradise. No bad books. No horrendous movies. No Phil Collins records. And certainly no T.G.I.F.–type cuisine. As we gradually wended our way south to rural Labecede, passing the days visiting cathedrals and reading books by Marcel Ayme and Jean Giono, I congratulated myself on my wise decision to flee the land of my birth. Clearly, my departure had delivered a shock to my psyche, with France serving as a kind of cultural sanitarium where I could cleanse my brain of the intellectual tuberculosis to which it had succumbed after my fatal encounter with Geraldo Rivera. Or something. With each passing day, my confidence increased, as my certainty grew that La Belle France was having the desired purgative effect, freeing me of my fetters of fealty to flapdoodle. To coin a phrase.

Then something disastrous occurred. There is a scene in the original version of *The Razor's Edge* where Gene Tierney leaves an open bottle of whiskey on a table in full view of Anne Baxter, her rival for Tyrone Power's affections, whom she knows to be a recovering alcoholic. Inevitably, Baxter starts drinking again, breaks off her engagement to Powers, and begins a long slide into the darkness of dipsomania. This is exactly what happened one afternoon when I walked into the living room to turn off the television that my children had been watching, and found an old episode of "Starsky and Hutch" flickering on the screen. Just for a giggle I sat down and watched the rest of the program, congratulating myself for finding it even more idiotic in French than in English. At the time, I merely thought how wonderful it was to be rid of my addiction to such plangent horseshit, and when the program ended I switched off the set.

But the next day, I rose early and while the rest of the family was still in bed, I sat riveted watching old, French-language reruns of "Matt Houston" and "Banacek." Then, feigning a headache, I waited until my family had wandered off to the beach before rushing back to the living room to catch both "T.J. Hooker" and "Remington Steele." I think I did a pretty good job of concealing my relapse from my family for the rest of the day, but that night I could not resist the urge to plant myself in front of the TV for a double feature of "Walker, Texas Ranger" and "Les Dessous de Palm Beach"

("Silk Stalkings"). By the time I went to bed that evening, I could no longer hide the truth from myself. The treatment had not taken effect. Once again, I was hooked.

I spent the next few days gallantly battling my addiction, but it was futile. Pretending to be out on a twenty-mile bike ride, I would actually steal into the forest with a copy of *Rich Man, Poor Man* plus an old Santana CD I found in my brother-in-law's otherwise impeccable collection. While my family visited eight-hundred-year-old churches and cathedrals dating from the days of the Knights Templar, I would stay behind in the village watching reruns of "The A-Team" and "Riptide." Things eventually got so bad that I found myself glued to the screen taking in an old series starring Connie Sellecca, to which the French had appended some absurd name. I had no idea what the original name of this series was, nor when it had originally aired. I only knew that Connie Sellecca was married to John Tesh, and that through this execrable program I could establish some ineffable psychic link with the Sultan of Suck, and thus get the daily cultural fix I so badly needed.

I was sinking, and I was sinking fast.

One afternoon my friends and family decided to visit Carcassonne, a mammoth walled city whose merchants would like tourists to believe that it dates from the time of the Romans, but which is actually a nineteenth-century reconstruction of a ruined medieval city, and thus almost a complete fake. The city does have an interesting mythology however: In the eighth century, it was besieged by Charlemagne and his vaunted horde of Franks. After many months of isolation, the city's residents finally ran out of food. Then a clever woman named Dame Carcas got a brilliant idea: to barbecue the last cow in the city, stuff it with dainty delights, and toss it over the walls of the city. This would deceive the invaders into thinking that the city was still well stocked with foodstuffs and give up the siege. The fact that this ploy worked shows you how stupid the Franks were. And the fact that American tourists believe this story shows that we really don't have all that much on the Franks. But Mrs. Carcas's ingenuity does explain the origin of the phrase, "There is nothing like a Dame."

Despite its somewhat spurious mythology, Carcassonne does in fact have an ancient church dating from the twelfth century and lots of other legitimate historical curiosities. None of this interested me. What interested me was sneaking off to attend a rehearsal of the medieval tournament held every afternoon in the shadow of the castle ramparts. This was an even bigger hoot than the Renaissance Faire in New York. The big knock on American medieval tournaments is that they conflate history by mixing costumes and customs from different countries and centuries. That, plus the fact that they're dumb. Central to this disdain for such anachronistic hijinks is the notion that when they put on these shows in Ye Olde Europe, they get things right.

Nonsense. "L'Enigme de 1237," a historical re-creation of the events taking place during the Albigensian Crusade of the thirteenth century, was the same load of crap as the Jerkwater Joustery I'd attended a few weeks earlier. The same insane continuity errors. The same greasers in leotards and bikinis masquerading as *chevaliers*. The same bony-assed locals trying to pass themselves off as comely wenches and saucy maidens. And I don't want to even mention the ubiquitous varlets, whoresons, and cutpurses. Suffice it to say that when the master of ceremonies made the announcement "Druids to the left, Visigoths to the right" and the soundtrack from the remake of *The Last of the Mohicans* welled up in the background, I knew I was in the presence of Franco-fakery of truly Fragonardian proportions.

And I loved every minute of it.

When, on August 6, 1997, I bought a copy of the *Herald Tribune* and read that Garth Brooks was giving his much ballyhooed free concert in Central Park the very next day, I doubled over in pain. What on earth had possessed me to leave New York City at the very moment that one of the true titans of lameness was rewarding his vast public with a once-in-a-lifetime experience, always to be cherished, never to be forgotten? What on earth had I been thinking?

That day, I frantically searched the local television listings to see if the concert would be carried live in the south of France. It would not. For one brief moment, I contemplated suicide. Then I thought I would perhaps arrange for a friend to attend the concert and call me on a public telephone, holding up the mouthpiece so I could hear a few bars of "Beaches of Cheyenne." Sadly, I realized that I didn't have any friends who would be seen dead at a Garth Brooks concert. I was on my own.

Garthless in Gaza, I realized what a pathetic shell of a man I had become. Pathetic, perhaps, but resourceful. For just then, when all hope had fled, a bolt of inspiration hit me. Lourdes was only a three-hour drive from Labecede, the village where I was staying. Perhaps, under the guise of enriching my children's education, I could persuade a couple of my friends to drive over to the famous French town. That way, I could visit the grotto where the Blessed Virgin Mary had appeared to Bernadette Soubirous in 1858, and beg her to cure my affliction. There were many cases on record in which people had been cured of blindness, leukemia, multiple sclerosis, and Epstein-Barr disease through the Virgin's intercession; perhaps the Blessed Mother could also cure what I had come to hope was in fact a major medical abnormality.

Lourdes, for the benefit of the uninitiated, is a French Niagara Falls. Unlike most major French cities, which usually have an ancient cathedral, an old castle, a viaduct, or a Roman amphitheater, Lourdes is a flat-out dump, a Wildwood, New Jersey, with more Catholics and fewer rides. It does have a basilica, but the basilica was built in the late nineteenth century and is hideous. Mostly, it consists of cheesy souvenir shops, tourist-trap hotels, and cruddy restaurants. The whole point of the Blessed Virgin appearing in such an out-of-the-way place was to reassure downtrodden French peasants that Jesus truly cared about them, and that the miraculous could occur not just in swish, trendy places like Jerusalem, Rome, and Paris but in shitholes like Lourdes. That the Blessed Virgin Mary would appear to an insignificant French teenager in this Gallic Podunk should give hope to the Chambers of Commerce in such no-account burgs as Altoona, Pennsylvania, and Gary, Indiana. Though personally, guys, I wouldn't hold your breath.

Arriving in Lourdes, I proceeded immediately to the famous grotto, where I joined a long line of pilgrims hoping to get a peek at the Virgin. The grotto wasn't much of a landmark—just a hole in the side of a hill—but let's face it, Plymouth Rock is nothing to write home about either. As I stood in line, attired in my John Tesh "The Avalon World Tour" T-shirt and clutching a copy of *Jonathan Livingston Seagull*, I explained the historical significance of this sacred locale to my daughter. I told her that, through the intercession of the Blessed Virgin Mary, the blind had been made to see, the deaf to hear, the lame to walk, the epileptic to get a grip. She wasn't buying it. She didn't see how any of this extraterrestrial rigamarole was going to be much help to a guy who couldn't go fifteen minutes without having to cue up "We Didn't Start the Fire" on the CD player. But she obligingly accompanied me as the line wound its way toward the grotto.

I am not going to tell you that I was struck by lightning when I entered the grotto. As grottos went, it was a bit of a dud, nothing like the ones you can find all over South Philadelphia. I'd been hoping for a deep, dank cave, when in fact the grotto was just a small crevice in the side of a small mountain. But when you are a guy blighted by the need to watch "Starsky and Hutch" reruns in French at eight o'clock in the morning, you can't afford to be fussy.

And, in truth, I definitely felt *something* as I prayed before the statue of the Virgin. As I begged Mother Mary to free me from bondage, I felt a gentle tingle of optimism surge through me. Perhaps She had heard my prayer. Perhaps I wouldn't be totally cured, but maybe my symptoms would at least diminish in severity. A blind man who would settle for restored vision in one eye, I mouthed the words:

"Blessed Mother of God, I am not worthy of your attention. This goes without saying. But if you could find it in the goodness of your heart to at least get this musical monkey off my back, I'd be beholden to you. I'd be more than happy to spend the rest of my days reading Tom Clancy books and going to see Liza Minnelli on Broadway. It's the music thing that's really busting my chops. I mean, look at this John Tesh T-shirt. If . . ."

I'd gotten about this far when the people right behind me started to surge forward, and I had to leave the grotto. I was miffed that I hadn't gotten a chance to finish my prayer. I felt like punching out the goddamn Italian tourists pressing on me from behind. But all in all I thought the Virgin had gotten the gist of my message. I wasn't asking for a major miracle. I was just asking for a little gesture of sympathy from above.

As I straggled out into the burning rays of the midday sun, I noticed a pile of medical apparatus that earlier pilgrims had left behind. Hanging from a wire were a bunch of canes and crutches. I also saw what I thought was a truss. Tearing open my CD holder, I pulled out my Kenny G compact disc and deposited it at the grotto's edge. The CD was the biggest-selling Christmas album of all time. It was entitled *Miracles*.

I hoped this was prophetic.

It wasn't prophetic. Although I bought a bunch of cheap plastic flasks and loaded them up with holy water, and drank about a gallon of the magic elixir before leaving Lourdes, I'd only gotten as far as the first café before I was faced with definitive evidence that the pilgrimage was a complete bust. While my daughter and my two French friends were off buying some profoundly ironic souvenirs they could take back to Amiens, I ducked into a café for a grand crème. On the jukebox, Abba was singing "Fernando," and within seconds I was singing along with them. When they were through singing "Fernando," I selected "Waterloo."

The cure hadn't worked; the curse was intact. As usual, I'd come to France seeking a respite from my daily travails, and as usual the French had fucked me right in the ear. Thanks a lot, frogs. Thanks a lot, Mary, Mother of Sorrows. Thanks a lot, God.

Into the Mystic

*I*n the middle of the night, I wake up screaming after suffering through a terrible nightmare. In the dream, a powerful organization called BOZO (Benign Order of Zenophobic
Oligopolists) is secretly planning to take over the United
States. Although the organization consists entirely of first-class
morons, the government fears its power so much that the FBI
has recruited me to infiltrate the shadowy group. I am not at
all taken with this idea, and somewhat puzzled, since the word
xenophobic is spelled with an x, not a z.

Phil and Stu, the FBI agents who have come to my house
to recruit me, are patient and understanding. They agree that
the word xenophobic is spelled with an x, but point out that
morons like the members of BOZO do not know how to spell.

"They're morons, Joe," Phil tells me. "They're lunkheads,
fuck-knuckles, shit-for-brains, assholes. But they're powerful."

Painstakingly, the agents map out the situation. For the
past twenty years, BOZO cadres have quietly been infiltrating
every milieu of American society. The evidence, though subtle,
is ubiquitous. Have I noticed the level of incompetence among

*salespeople in this country these days? That's because the in-
telligent personnel have all been forced out or murdered by
members of BOZO. Ever notice how stupid security guards
are? I have. BOZO's work again, the agents inform me. Ever
try to buy an airplane ticket? Ever notice that no cashier in
America can change register tape without divine intervention?
Ever been to the post office? That's right, in each and every
case, the dark shadow of BOZO has eclipsed the bright sun of
competence.*

*Little by little, brick by brick, Phil and Stu build their
case. Haven't I ever noticed that my kids' textbooks don't seem
to be quite up to snuff? I have. BOZO, they explain. Have I
noticed that the Senate is teeming with morons like Al
D'Amato and Strom Thurmond? BOZO. Have I noticed that
television, radio, and the media are dominated by dunces like
Rush Limbaugh, Jenny Jones, and Barbara Walters? The spec-
ter of BOZO.*

*Eventually, I realize that this BOZO conspiracy is no
laughing matter. What I still don't understand is why they've
come to me. After all, I'm a sophisticated, educated, well-read
kind of guy. What makes them think I could pass for a member
of BOZO?*

*"We've been keeping a tail on you for the past ten months,
Joe," says Stu. "We know that you've seen Kenny G and John
Tesh in concert. We know that you've been to see Victor/Vic-
toria three times. We have photographs of you reading* Men
Are from Mars, Women Are from Venus *and* The Horse
Whisperer. *And we know that on at least two occasions you've
dined at T.G.I.F. We're not saying that you're a moron, Joe.
But for the past ten months, you've sure been acting like one."*

*I try to explain that I'm researching a book. They merely
chuckle.*

"Right, like the guy who screws four-year-olds because he's

writing a book on child abuse," says Phil. "Like the guy who wears diapers and a pacifier because he's writing about infantilism. Sorry, pal. Been there, done that."

I can see that there is no point in arguing with them. Moreover, I am a patriotic American, ready to do whatever is necessary to keep the home fires burning, despite the rockets' red glare. But even after an intense ten-month submersion in the very worst of American culture, I still feel and look like an intelligent person. More to the point, the extent of my expertise in the whole subculture of shitheadedness, though mammoth by the standards of the intelligent people I normally hang around with, is still rather superficial.

"We understand that," says Phil. "And before we send you undercover, you'll undergo a six-week intensive shitheaded orientation program just to make sure you have at least a passing knowledge of everything a normal American moron would need to know. By the time we're through with you, you'll not only know who won the 1997 NASCAR Winston Cup ITW DeVilbiss 400 and who wrote the riff that Yanni reworks on "Aria" from Live at the Acropolis, *but what kind of sky Jake Cantrell saw on the first page of Barbara Taylor Bradford's* Love in Another Town.*"*

Actually, I already know the answers to those questions. Mark Martin won the 1997 NASCAR Winston Cup ITW DeVilbiss 400. Yanni borrowed the riff on "Aria" from the nineteenth-century French composer Leo Delibes. And the sky that Jake Cantrell saw on the first page of Barbara Taylor Bradford's Love in Another Town *was etiolated. In fact, it was "so bleached out it, too, seemed as pale and as unmoving as the water." What's more, I am probably one of the few people in the United States with a three-digit IQ who knows that Maggie, the woman Jake dumped his first wife for, because theirs was a loveless marriage, had breasts that were perfect.*

That is, *"softly rounded, with smooth and pale skin"*—like the babes' at Hooters. I suppose it is the ease with which I answer these questions that convinces me to accept this dangerous assignment. From the looks of it, this is going to be a piece of cake.

For the next six weeks I attend moron indoctrination class for fourteen hours a day at a secret government compound located somewhere in the Deep South. I am only allowed to sleep three hours a night, never more than forty-five minutes a time, and am dragged out of bed at all hours of the day and brutally interrogated by Navy SEALs:

"What is the Sicilian term for a son who refuses to follow his father's bidding in a Mario Puzo novel?" they demand.

"A figlio disgraziato," I reply.

"In what movie did Mitzi Kapture, the original star of 'Silk Stalkings,' appear with the vastly underrated Maud Adams?"

"Angel III," I respond.

"How much is the salad bar at the Sizzler in Yonkers, New York?"

"When purchased with another meal, $2.99; when purchased on its own, $7.99. But everyone just goes up and serves themselves anyway."

"Under what jurisdiction did the civilians in Tom Clancy's Op-Center: Acts of War *go into enemy territory and rescue the hero from his bloodthirsty Kurdish captors?"*

I have to think about that one for a minute. Then it comes to me.

"According to Lowell Coffey, it was Section 17, Subsection 2, B-1-a-1, which gave them, as civilians, the right to go in and get Mike out. The question they'd wrestled with en route was whether bringing Colonel Seden out constituted a partisan act. Because he was a Turkish soldier who had entered the region with partisan interest, he was not covered by Section

17, Subsection 2, B-1-a-2. However, Coffey said that as long as the colonel was hurt, his evacuation would be acceptable in accordance with the charter of the International Red Cross. According to Section 8, Subsection 3, A-1-b-3, ROC was permitted to act under the IRC charter to evacuate wounded outsiders at the discretion of the individual in charge."

Even the SEALs are impressed by that performance.

Upon completing my indoctrination program, I am given a new identity and a job where I am likely to be contacted by members of BOZO. I figure it will probably involve posing as a pinspotter in a rural Oklahoma bowling alley for the blind or as a ski instructor in Bedford-Stuyvesant, but no, I am named program director for MTV. Scant days after I assume the position, I am contacted by BOZO. I am blindfolded and taken to one of their top-secret meetings at Barbra Streisand's house.

As soon as I arrive, I realize just how great a threat to American society this nefarious organization poses. For years, I have assumed that the most famous morons in our society are independent operators, free-booters who carve their own niche and go their own way. But when I walk into the room and see Madonna chatting with Jackie Collins, and the entire cast of Lord of the Dance *hopping up and down while John Tesh tinkles the ivories and Kenny G wails away on his sax in the background while Chuck Norris hoists a few brewskies with Roseanne, I realize that they are all in this together. Yes, it is a conspiracy. While Tori Spelling and Jerry Springer launch a diversionary frontal assault on American civilization, Geraldo Rivera and Danielle Steel sweep in from the flanks, catching the public in a classic pincers movement. Meanwhile, Regis and Kathie Lee seal off the last avenue of escape.*

Involuntarily, I start to gag.

Suddenly, I am surrounded by sinister security forces dressed entirely in black. They bind and gag me, drag me into a subterranean torture chamber, and begin the interrogation.

"Why did David Hasselhoff have such a falling out with his father on 'Baywatch'?" the ringleader demands.

"Because Mitch wanted to pursue a career as a full-time lifeguard and his dad wanted him to be an architect," I reply.

"Who plays piano on Billy Joel's song 'Piano Man' on the 1975 LP Piano Man?" he asks.

"I believe that would be Billy Joel," I answer.

"What does Della Reese do with her spare time in 'Promised Land' when she's not helping out Roma Downey?"

This is a trick question. No one knows the answer to that. And that's the way I handle it.

"She just disappears, and no one knows where she goes," I reply. "For all I know she may secretly be out looking for those Colombian drug dealers who killed Nicole Brown Simpson."

A malevolent smile surges across my interrogator's face.

"That's correct, Mr. Queenan. No one knows what Della Reese does with her spare time when she's not helping out Roma Downey."

His lip curls in a sinister fashion.

"But Della Reese does not appear with Roma Downey on 'Promised Land.' She appears every Sunday night on 'Touched by an Angel,' the show that made Ms. Downey famous. Something any moron would know."

And then he reaches for the white-hot branding iron and pries open my right eyelid.

★　★　★

Upon my return from France, I reverted to my old ways. Even when I awoke, the nightmare would not pass. My days found me prowling the streets seeking out fresh horrors. I purchased Pat Boone's heavy-metal album, *No More Mr. Nice Guy* and snapped up a couple of moldy Gallagher videos. One afternoon I went to see a Shaquille O'Neal movie. After the film, I wandered over to the Motown Café on West 57th Street, where every half-hour a quintet of young men masquerading as the Temptin' Temptations took the stage and sang one of the chartbusters' greatest hits. I listened to "Beauty's Only Skin Deep" while eating tepid southern fried chicken with a side order of macaroni and steamed zucchini. Whose idea of soul food was this?

In the downstairs bathroom, I took a piss and was greeted by a young black man who offered me a towel. It is no secret that the only job in the United States that is worse than being the Shithouse Greeter is being the Vice President of the United States, who is, for all intents and purposes, the White House Shithouse Greeter. Didn't the Motown Café, of all the establishments in New York, realize that it's a bit tacky to have a young black man working in the bathroom, handing out towels to guys who only recently were manipulating their meat? Wasn't there some kind of weird symbolism here? Couldn't they have gotten some desperate cracker to do the job instead? If we were, in point of fact, a-movin' on up, shouldn't we also have been a-movin' on *out*?

And yet, there was a part of me that reveled in such bad taste.

As was usually the case, it was my musical excursions that took me to the deepest, dankest regions of the underworld. One night I found myself at Radio City Music Hall, jiggling my hips and clapping my hands to the infectious Latin beat of the Gipsy Kings. I had come to Radio City this evening because throughout the late 1980s and 1990s it was impossible to go to any hip restaurant in the New York area without hearing the hyperfrantic strumming and yelping of these pop flamenco maestros. In my mind, the Gipsy Kings were inextricably linked with Key lime pie, fresh angel hair pasta with just a touch of pesto sauce, and overpriced polenta. Seeing them in person for the first time, I realized that the Gipsy Kings are basically just Flamenco Abba, with a rhythmic range that is narrower than the Beach Boys and a stage presence that is pure Ricardo Montalban. They are, in every sense of the word, the musical equivalent of the finest Corinthian leather.

Yet, when the audience rose as one to sing "Volare" toward the end of the show, I was chanting and swaying just as merrily as the rest of the crowd, gazing out upon this ocean of losers and saying to myself: "These are my people."

Unfortunately, I said the very same thing to myself at an Emerson, Lake and Palmer concert two nights later, and that's when I knew that I was a complete goner. I had been a party to innumerable musical crimes in my lifetime—I saw the hopelessly juvenile Frank Zappa seven times, I saw Iron Butterfly twice, I owned the first two Steppenwolf albums, and I even bought *Frampton Comes Alive!*—but I had always managed to resist the siren song of these overwrought, artsy-fartsy, Rimsky-Korsakov-Meets-Yes metalheads. Yet now, at the ripe old age of forty-six, I was at the Beacon Theatre, a guest at the show that (literally) never ends, reveling in the smoke, the cheesy light show, the gongs, the pseudo-regal drum flourishes, the wheezy Moog Synthesizer, the butchered Aaron Copland selections, the whole faux-classical art-rock *Krapperdämmerung*.

But it was only when I actually heard myself chanting, "Oooh, what a lucky man he wassss!!! Oooh, what a lucky man he wassss!!!" along with a portly, balding Greg Lake and a roomful of art-rock burnouts that I realized the full implications of my behavior: Edward Hyde had now taken over complete dominion of my personality, and I was in this thing way, way too deep. I had finally, irreversibly lost the plot, and it was time to get some professional help.

Although it will come as a shock to those who have always known me as a deeply nonspiritual person, by the time September 1997 came rolling around, I was more than ready to embrace the intercession of the mystical, the paranormal, or the divine if it would help release me from my own special brand of insanity. My friends said that if I was sincere about seeking help from my Greater Power, I should consider attending unorthodox religious services. Unfortunately, I'd already tried that, and my faith in organized religions had long since worn thin.

Believe me, I'm not just talking about Lourdes. Although raised as a Catholic, I had avoided church services for several years because of an unsettling experience I'd had back in 1992. While researching a story for *GQ* about ludicrous religious services, I had attended the Blessing of the Animals on the Feast of St. Francis at an Episcopalian church in White Plains, New York, about five miles from my home. The service was a dire affair, complete with a guitar-strumming cleric afflicted with a serious case of guitar face, but the worst part was the blessing itself. The minister blessed cats. He blessed dogs. He blessed parakeets. He blessed snakes. But he also blessed ferrets, hamsters, assorted rodents, and even cute little teddy bears. I found it very hard to concentrate during the service because the woman sitting next to me had what appeared to be an iguana poised on her left shoulder, dangerously close to my face.

This, I believe, is probably the biggest difference between

Catholics and Episcopalians, who in most other respects have very similar beliefs. Episcopalians do not believe in the Immaculate Conception. Catholics do. Episcopalians do not believe in the infallibility of the pope. Catholics do. But Episcopalians do apparently believe in the redemptive capacities of iguanas, which Catholics do not. You don't tend to see many reptiles at Roman Catholic religious services. Not unless you count local Irish pols scrounging for votes.

I found the iguana's presence so annoying that I eventually asked the woman to move the repellent reptile to the other shoulder. She glared at me with the kind of high dudgeon you tend to associate with plump, middle-aged Earth Mothers who subscribe to *Mother Jones* and for a time honestly believed that Dan Quayle was the second coming of Lucifer.

"It's not an iguana," she snapped, sizing me up quickly as a guy who didn't spend a lot of his free time watching rebroadcasts of ancient David Attenborough specials on the Discovery Channel. "It's a monitor."

"I don't care what it is," I fired back. "Put your pet Gila monster on the other shoulder or I'm going to get you thrown out of here."

After the ceremony, I approached the minister who had conducted this bizarre service and asked if the blessing of teddy bears and other inanimate objects was not committing the sin of simony or one of those other highly technical ecclesiastical transgressions I used to read about when I was an altar boy in grade school. He blew me off with a knowing smile that seemed to say, "Lighten up, my son."

This was the last time I seriously considered becoming Episcopalian. And Lourdes pretty much put the kabosh on Catholicism. Judaism, lacking a serious mumbo-jumbo side, didn't seem to have much to offer here either, so I decided to turn to inspirational literature as a way out of my dilemma. My first stop was *The Road Less Traveled*, an immensely popular book about spiritual growth that made an awful lot of sense for the first 150 pages until M. Scott Peck suddenly, inexplicably began quoting from first-class chuckleheads like Kahlil Gibran and John Denver. There was also a really scary part where Peck talks about a morbid patient who began to see all the good, happy, right things in life after he started listening to *Jesus Christ, Superstar* and *Godspell* and bought a copy of *Jonathan Livingston Seagull*.

Here we arrive at one of the biggest problems in contemporary self-help literature: the fatal decision to select contemporary role models as inspirational figures without realizing how pathetic these people may seem just a few years down the road less traveled. In Peck's case, an otherwise excellent book is tragically wounded by the foolish decision to cite not only the aforementioned John Denver, Kahlil Gibran, and Andrew Lloyd Webber, but also the mystical ding-dong Carlos Castaneda. Personally, I think he would have been much better off sticking with proven longball hitters like Leo Tolstoy, Dante, René Descartes. And Jesus Christ, as opposed to Jesus Christ, Superstar.

But Peck was not the only author to succumb to the siren song of fleeting hipness. *I'm OK, You're OK*, an influential but unreadable book, cites the wisdom of one Timothy Leary, making it all that much less readable. And in his vastly influential 1986 book *Unlimited Power*, infomercial king Anthony Robbins provides an excellent road map for getting one's life under control, then undercuts his own arguments with similar star-gazing. Things start off well enough, with the toothsome motivator explaining how, through the judicious placement of emotional anchors, the careful utilization of metaprograms, and serious attention to submodalities, a person can literally teach himself how to walk across a bed of hot coals. Or, for that matter, read the complete works of Harold Robbins.

But then Robbins hijacks his own argument by anointing Pete Rose, now banned from major league baseball, as a role model, and by speaking in rapt terms of such widely discredited individuals as Lee Iacocca and Steve Jobs. When you choose Alexander the Great and Julius Caesar as your idols, you really can't go wrong. But contemporary heroes always have skeletons in the closet or bats in the belfry or Bruno Magli loafers in the shoe rack, making the book seem preposterous just a few years after it appears. Look at Marv Albert.

The exact same thing happened when I read Gail Sheehy's mammoth mid-seventies best-seller *Passages*. Although Sheehy goes a bit heavy on catch phrases like the Trying Twenties, The Deadline Decade, Breaking Away from the Inner Custodian, Closed-Dyad Disease, Paranurturers, Latency Boys, Late Baby Superachievers, and the Urge to Merge, I was willing to give her the benefit of the doubt because her arguments about the uniqueness of the midlife crisis are so persuasive. *Hey, it certainly seemed like I was having one.* But then, late in the book, the whole ball of wax collapses when Sheehy recounts the story of a powerful executive's epic voyage of self-discovery.

The man, in Sheehy's words, "had a father who made him feel powerless, who left the family floundering financially and emotionally when the boy was young." But he grew up to become a corporate titan, a man with an unconquerable dream. "Everything about it was predicated on the image of himself as physically strong, mentally fleet, emotionally fearless, and on his way to becoming all-powerful." And, by the by, reports Sheehy, the man was "genuine in describing his rising need to make a social contribution," to give something back to society. The man's name? John DeLorean.

Nevertheless, my thirst for wisdom, for the balm of Gilead, did not stop there. I tried watching Bill Moyers's "Genesis," but it was just no use; it took Moyers ten hours to say what God had said in about two. Then I turned to Andrew Weil's best-seller *Spontaneous Healing*. Perhaps through cranial therapy, massive vitamin E supplements, yoga, massage, psychic healing, or simply eating a lot of brown rice I could rid myself of my passion for piffle. One other suggestion was that I "regard my illness as a gift," that instead of viewing my cultural cancer as an invasive disease, I begin to regard it as a part of me that I must love. But that night I went home and read both *All I Really Need to Know I Learned in Kindergarten* and *Chicken Soup for the Soul*. Robert Fulghum likes to rhapsodize about the emotional appeal of Crayola crayons and draws lessons from the exploits of the eensy-weensy spider. *Chicken Soup for the Soul* includes poems by Kahlil Gibran and implausible anecdotes about cheerful bag ladies. It was impossible for me to love *that* cancer. Not yet, at least. Geraldo hadn't taken *complete* control.

I suppose it was inevitable that, like so many members of my generation, I would finally turn to the mystical east for help. Specifically, I turned to Deepak Chopra. Not so many months earlier, my local PBS station decided to broadcast a program entitled "Deepak Chopra: The Way of the Wizard" during its semiannual pledge week. Chopra, an Indian-born physician who was once chief of staff at New England Memorial Hospital, was now a full-time seer who preached that all of us must locate the wizard within us in order to take the next great leap of faith which would lead to the process of metabiological evolution that would enable us to realize that death is not a tragic event but just another form of consciousness.

I had first been exposed to the work of Mr. Chopra in October 1991, when I attended the First International Men's Conference in Austin, Texas. This was a horribly undignified event at which 765 grown men openly wept, chanted songs to obscure West African deities, engaged in something called mythopoetic dancing, and blamed their fathers for everything that had ever befallen them in the course of their shabby lives. In a magazine piece, I had suggested at the time that all of these men badly needed to be executed, with their mangled corpses deposited in shallow graves so roving hyenas could dig up their remains and have a bit of a snack.

Although Chopra was not present at this event, his books and audiotapes were on sale, right alongside bizarre motivational materials with such titles as *Warming the Stone Child*, *Demystifying the Wise Woman/Crone*, and *Stale Roles & Tight Buns: Images of Men in Advertising*. As an ardent believer in the concept of guilt by association, I decided at the time that Chopra must be every bit as dreadful as the rest of these drum-toting whiners. Thus, I was greatly incensed when my PBS station preempted its regular Sunday night programming of simpering Edwardian butlers wooing repressed women in crinoline to instead present "The Way of the Wizard."

The program began in predictably horrifying fashion, with that obligatory sitar, flute, and tambour music that invariably signals that we are in the presence of mystic seers, wisdom-drenched shamans, or George Harrison. Then Chopra, a pudgy, middle-aged, New Age megaguru, appeared in the middle of a courtyard in front of a bunch of well-heeled yuppies and began talking about his childhood hero, Merlin. (Mine was Merlin Olsen.) Eventually, the subject turned to the really big questions of human existence. Basically, Chopra's spiel ran like this: Death was merely nature's way of getting people to think about Life in a totally different way.

"When you know that Death is stalking you . . ." Chopra told his awed listeners, "your life will become magical."

This was Deepak Chopra quoting Carlos Casteneda, at his most lucid. But there was another segment in "The Way of the Wizard" where he said: "But now a stage comes when the seeker is born into the seer. Because the seeker has discovered that that which the seeker was seeking was the seeker and having sought the seeker, it has become the seer." Even Deepak had a hard time keeping a straight face when presenting this kind of material.

Drawing upon luminaries as varied as Emily Dickinson, Friedrich Nietzsche, T. S. Eliot, Hermann Hesse, and Rabindranath Tagore, Mr. Chopra contended that none of us could achieve a state of perfect happiness until we had escaped the "prison of the known" and come to a realization that death is merely our "wedding with eternity." He also likened life to a child sucking on his mother's right breast, while death was very much like a child sucking on his mother's left breast.

At the time, his spiel struck me as a replay of the Inscrutable Orient's Meets Bill Moyers's Greatest Hits: reincarnation, cosmic oneness, passive acceptance of the inevitable—your basic Firesign Theater material. Viewed in this light, it was easy to write off PBS's broadcasting decision as a harmless way of tapping into aging boomers' passion for all that sixties Electric Prunes stuff. So at the time I turned off the TV and thought no more about it.

But a few months after my tragic encounter with Geraldo

Rivera, I found myself discussing Mr. Chopra's philosophy with a female friend. Basically, I said that my antipathy to Mr. Chopra was an East-West thing, and felt that the best way to decide the issue was to go to the scoreboard. The way I saw it, we had Plato, Letterman, capitalism, Mozart, Springsteen, zero coupon bonds, and Michael Jordan on our side of the ledger, and they had Buddha, Ravi Shankar, and Deepak Chopra. So we won, hands down.

Then my friend said something interesting. She'd seen "The Way of the Wizard," and generally admired Chopra's work. Nevertheless, she admitted that the program did not show this modern Merlin at his best. She asserted that Chopra's greatest contribution to contemporary thought was his notion that human intellect could be used to triumph over the aging process, and particularly over physical maladies such as heart disease, cancer, and even AIDS. She suggested that I read his book *Ageless Body, Timeless Mind*, which predated "The Way of the Wizard" and had sold more than 2 million copies. She also said that I should take a peek at his video *Explorations into Consciousness*.

At this point, I was willing to try anything, so I eagerly bought the book and tape, as well as *The Seven Spiritual Laws of Success*. I hadn't gotten very far into them before I realized that my friend was right—that I'd been selling Chopra short. In *Ageless Body, Timeless Mind,* Chopra explained how it was possible for a human being to cure his own diseases simply by "reinterpreting" his body. And in *Explorations into Consciousness*, he explained how it was possible to "activate the self-healing mechanism in human beings" by tapping into the greatest pharmacy the world has ever known: the self-renewing, self-regenerating, self-healing "quanta" that exist inside every human being.

In other words, it was possible for sick people to heal themselves just by getting that goddamn chip off their shoulder.

"I have many patients with AIDS who are healthier than most people walking down the street," Chopra beamed out from my TV screen. "They haven't had a cold in five years."

From that moment on, I devoured everything I could find by Deepak Chopra. The shift in my world view was dramatic. By surrendering my list of desires to the womb of creation, I gradually came to see that he was right, that my body really was a flute through whose heart the whispering of the hours turns to music. I also now recognized the fundamental difference between me and a tree. Basically, there is no difference. Or, as Chopra puts it: "The only difference between you and a tree is the informational and energy content of your respective bodies." This is also the only difference between me, a tree, and Dennis Rodman.

I gained a profound personal insight when I went back and reviewed *Explorations into Consciousness*. This is the tape where Chopra argues that while cancer patients may not actually "choose" their disease, they may in fact "participate in it." This would certainly apply to me. I'd walked right into this disease. I had embraced it.

But it was in the classic *The Seven Spiritual Laws of Success* that Deepak put his finger on my problem. "Judgment," he wrote, "is the constant evaluation of things as right or wrong, good or bad. When you are constantly evaluating, classifying, labeling, analyzing, you create a lot of turbulence in your internal dialogue."

That sentence hit me like a shot to the solar plexus. All this time I'd been barking up the wrong tree. I didn't need to be *cured* of my disease; I needed to give in to it. And I could do this by simply lightening up. My entire adult life I had been a hyperkinetically judgmental person. I had earned my living by making sneering, vicious comments about the likes of John Tesh, Michael Bolton, Liza Minnelli, KISS. From now on, I decided, I would take Deepak Chopra's advice to heart. "Today, I shall judge nothing that occurs," he advised. From here on out, I would stop being judgmental. I would merely act as a spectator in my own life. Hopefully, I would come to realize that the goal of life was not to think, the goal of life was merely to be.

And it was time for me to be somewhere other than New York.

He Wore Blue Velvet

When I started out on the Highway to Hell back in March 1996, I had honestly assumed that the realm of the repugnant was infinite, that no one, in one lifetime, could ever make it through all the bad books, bad movies, bad restaurants, bad plays, bad music, and bad ideas that this culture had produced. Technically speaking, this was true. What I hadn't realized was that the realm of the *unspeakably* repugnant did not approach the infinite, and that its resources could be exhausted in a relatively short period of time. In my case, in about twelve months.

This was a serious issue for me, because the unspeakably repugnant had now become the lifeblood of my existence, and my reserves were running low. I had seen every Adam Sandler movie, listened to every Billy Joel CD, read the complete works of O. J. Simpson. And now the larder was bare. Throughout my experiences, I had consistently drawn a distinction between the evanescently crappy and the institutionally idiotic. This was the distinction between flashes-in-the pan like Menudo, Vanilla Ice, Milli Vanilli, Joe Piscopo, and

Pauly Shore, all of whom held a brief stranglehold over this society and then disappeared, and sea serpents like Kenny G, Barbra Streisand, and Stephen King, who coiled themselves around the public's guts at an early age and never let go.

While my mind could grasp this concept, my flesh was weak and I found that my gargantuan appetite for the genuinely horrendous, the stupefyingly awful, could not be sated by a mere snack. A stomach grown accustomed to feasting on John Tesh, Robert Ludlum, and Andrew Lloyd Webber could not settle for a meal consisting of the Spice Girls, Fran Drescher, and Celine Dion. Like a tiger who has tasted human flesh for the first time, my eating habits had been changed forever. I needed big game—and only big game.

In short, Deepak Chopra wasn't going to be any help, after all.

It was chilling testimony to the intensity of my addiction that Las Vegas could not provide the fix I was looking for. I had never visited Las Vegas in the first forty-six years of my existence because I had always assumed that it would be repulsive and depressing. It was not. Vegas was astonishingly middle class and ordinary. With its vast theme hotels bearing names like Excalibur and Treasure Island, Las Vegas was teeming with average Americans at all hours of the day and night. There was gambling galore and there was sleaze to be found, but the sleaze was not apparent to the naked eye (no hookers working the strip), and the gambling did not spill out onto the streets. The most amazing thing about Las Vegas was how comfortable the whole thing felt. I had come here expecting it to be *pathetic,* and instead it was merely *absurd.* Absurdity wasn't going to cut it for me.

For the aficionado of High Suck, Las Vegas was just too

wholesome. As I quickly discovered by talking to cabdrivers, over the past decade the city had essentially converted itself into a vast, urban theme park suitable for the whole family. I had envisioned a somewhat tawdry mixture of Times Square and Atlantic City, teeming with prostitutes and gangsters. It was nothing of the sort. Instead, it was swarming with gaggles of thoroughly normal-looking Americans in shorts and sunglasses off for a week in the sun. This town used to be for Goodfellas. Now it was for good fellows. I had expected it to look like Sodom. Instead, it looked like Epcot.

I am not suggesting that my trip to Las Vegas was an entire waste of time. The medieval banquet at the Excalibur, hosted by a crotchety old Merlin who was more varmint than sorcerer, was a bona fide suckfest. The knight's retainers, in thongs and leotards, showed too much thigh and the winsome maidens not nearly enough. Haberdashery was also a problem up at Caesar's Palace: With its toga-clad centurions and mysterious gladiators, the hotel/casino looked like a set from a direct-to-video movie starring Richard Simmons with a screenplay by Truman Capote. But mammoth hotels like Treasure Island and the MGM Grand were merely outlandish, not idiotic. Las Vegas had some sort of context.

The big problem with Las Vegas was that it had a sense of its own absurdity. With its tiger cages, shark tanks, and Secret Garden of Siegfried and Roy, the Mirage Hotel was cognizant of its own garish, over-the-top personality. The same was true of the Luxor, with its cheesy reproduction of the Sphinx and its $5.99 Pharoah's Pheast. Yes, Las Vegas was preposterous. But it was preposterous in the way Michael Jackson was preposterous. It was preposterous, but it wasn't stupid.

The place that best defines the city's personality is the Liberace Museum. Located at the edge of a large strip mall about two miles from downtown Las Vegas, the Liberace Museum is run by a couple of affable senior citizens. The bejeweled clothing, cars, and pianos on display in the museum are all tawdry and excessive, like the man who once owned them. But there is nothing overtly pathetic about Liberace or his ornamentation. I suppose this is because Liberace, both in life and death, literally got away with murder, evolving into a national treasure by butchering the classics for an audience of senior citizens who obstinately refused to believe that he was gay. When you look at the photograph of Liberace shaking hands with an obviously bewildered Ronald Reagan, you cannot help but admire a man who could successfully execute a lifelong gag of such spectacular proportions. Liberace gave the American people what they wanted, and in return got what he wanted—an odd sort of immortality. He stayed on top; his aura never faded; he never ended up playing tank towns in Central Arkansas at the end of his career. A classically trained musician churning out unadulterated cornpone, he pulled off the crime of the century.

Liberace is the spiritual father of Las Vegas, with Tubby Elvis its uncle. Because it knows what it is, it cannot be criticized for being what it isn't. Nowhere was this made more abundantly clear for me than when I purchased the very last ticket available for Wayne Newton's final show of the season at the MGM Grand. I need not explain who Wayne Newton is, nor what he has represented to me for most of my adult life. Nor do I need to explain why I bought that last ticket. In fact, I would be lying if I did not come right out and admit that I had come to Las Vegas with but one purpose in mind: to see Wayne Newton live, on stage, on his own turf. Not at some godforsaken summer music fair under a Long Island tent. Not at some forlorn Connecticut casino. Not in Atlantic City, an out-and-out hellhole. No, when you go to see the King of Schmaltz, you go to see him in his kingdom.

Wayne Newton would prove even more of a surprise to me than Barry Manilow had six months earlier. Scant minutes into his act, I realized the merit of the axiom: "Be careful what you wish for." For most of my life, I had shared my entire generation's fervent wish that lounge lizards like Wayne Newton would disappear from the face of the earth so that rock 'n' roll could rule the planet. So now we had Marilyn Manson and Snoop Doggy Dog. As I watched Newton, one of the last of the great lounge lizards, working with all engines a-throttle, I realized that our baby-boomer wish had essentially come true and that once again we had wrecked things for everybody.

Just as my parents had rued the passing of vaudeville, with its irreplaceable Ritz Brothers and Rudy Vallees, I now rued the passing of the lounge lizards of yore. When they were gone, there would be no more popping of cuffs, no more undone bow ties, no more black female back-up singers going "ooh" and "ah." Instead, there would be spindly young men in flannel shirts playing recycled Byrds songs, mopers and whiners who couldn't make eye contact with the audience if their lives depended on it. And, oh yes, gangstas. Plus an ocean of interchangeable stand-up comics. Once, show biz had been dominated by the likes of Tom Jones, Engelbert Humperdinck, Wayne Newton. Now, the kingdom was passing into the hands of Huey Lewis & the News, Eddie Money, Howie Mandel.

This was progress?

The Wayne Newton show was a two-hour affair of uninterrupted, uncompromising, unapologetic Vegas glitz. First, Newton appeared in a cloud of smoke at the top of a staircase as the band churned out *Also sprach Zarathustra*. Then he belted out a couple of Elvis hits. Then he engaged in some good-natured banter with the audience. Then some mildly risqué jokes; Captain, a bottle of champagne for the woman in the eighteenth row; more Elvis hits; cuff-popping; struts; a tribute to his wife; eyes rolling to the heavens in heartfelt appreciation for the crowd's support; some wise-cracks about being an Indian; tai-chi kicks; airborne panties; a Wayno guitar solo; some impersonations; an off-the-cuff rendition of "MacArthur Park"; a Wayno piano solo; a pair of anachronistic black tap dancers; Wayno's banjo version of "Waitin' on the Robert E. Lee." Then, finally, inevitably, a moving version of Elvis's "American Trilogy," at the end of which Newton disappeared back up the stairs, into the smoke, and vaporized.

If there was a dry eye in the house, I didn't see it.

I was willing to believe, as I had been willing to believe six months earlier at Barry Manilow's Radio City concert, that Newton impressed me so much because my over-exposure to pap had shipwrecked my critical acumen. But in truth, I didn't buy it. Newton, like Manilow, like Jerry Lewis, like Don Rickles, like Mel Tormé, was an old trouper, and you had to love an old trouper. You had to love an old trouper because old troupers give until there is nothing left to give. They sweat, they churn, they mojo, they gyrate, they truck, they boogie, they mambo, they get in the groove, they jack it up a few notches, they swear that if this don't turn you on, you ain't got no switches. Old troupers know that even before they have begun, it is too late to stop now.

My problem was that I hadn't come to Las Vegas to see someone I would come away admiring. I had come to see someone who sucked beyond all measure, someone who sucked worse than anyone had a right to suck. Debbie Reynolds was not that person. Siegfried and Roy did not fill that bill, nor did their sexually ambivalent tigers. The guys and gals at the Folies-Bergère show were not down to that particular snuff. In the past, I had been successful in mixing several low-rent experiences (a bad book, a bad meal, a bad movie, a bad record) into a "Suck Cocktail," whose cumulative effects equaled that of one big, bad Broadway show. But now I needed something a little stronger than a cocktail. I needed the cultural equivalent of 151-proof, rancid tequila.

Luckily for me, David Cassidy was in town. David Cassidy is the ostensible star of a show called *EFX*, though the real stars of the show are the special effects themselves. The show, replete with aircraft, dragons, time machines, and underwater machinery would be enough to dwarf the talents of even the mightiest performer, but Cassidy's talents need precious little dwarfing. An ineffective singer and incompetent dancer, Cassidy is America's last link with a past it cannot remember because it probably never happened. In this eye-popping extravaganza, he plays an ordinary mortal who is somehow given the opportunity to go back in time and correct the mistakes of his past. Like ever working with Danny Bonaduce. The show is a Götterdämmerung of sound and fury, with everyone from P. T. Barnum to H. G. Wells to Merlin to Harry Houdini turning up to take a bow. Its hootiness is not to be believed. Indeed, its hootiness is of such an extravagant nature that when narrator James Earl Jones's huge face appears on a massive screen or a hologram or a laser beam or whatever at the beginning of the program, Jones himself seems to be having difficulty keeping a straight face. James Earl Jones, who isn't even on stage at any point during the show, can't resist snickering at Cassidy's antics. It is that bad.

The most satisfying development in the whole lurid spectacle the evening I saw it occurred when Cassidy picked a young woman out of the crowd and asked her to come up on stage. Her job was to pretend to be his long-lost girlfriend, Laura, for the remainder of the show. But wouldn't you know that Cassidy selected the one female in the crowd who had no interest whatsoever in sharing a stage with David Cassidy. She may not have even known who he was. *Like, he's not Marky Mark.* No matter how earnestly he pleaded with her to go along with the gag, to cut him some slack, to give him a fucking break, the cold-assed bitch remained recalcitrantly uncooperative, stiff as a board.

"Laura, Laura, why don't you speak to me?" he asked, frustrated.

"Because my name's not Laura," she replied.

At this point you realized why David Cassidy did not belong in the same town, much less the same business, as a titan like Wayne Newton. Had Wayne Newton been handling this situation, he would have worked the old show-biz magic, gotten the young woman to settle down, cajoled her into cooperating. Either that, or he would have called for another volunteer from the audience. That's the way Don Rickles would have handled it. That's the way Jerry Lewis would have handled it. For all I know, that's the way Ricardo Montalban would have handled it.

But Cassidy was not in the same league as those lords of the boards. So he did the worst thing imaginable: He let her stay on stage for the entire remainder of the show. For the next half-hour, perhaps longer, Cassidy valiantly struggled to make the show soar while "Laura" kept him hopelessly tethered to the ground. If the woman hadn't been such a stiff, the climactic scene where she was chained to a rock by a gang of scantily clad Amazon warriors could have been fun. *You know, maybe get some lesbo action going.* But Not-Laura would have none of it. No Betty Page she, "Laura" looked about as fetching in Sapphic cannibal bondage as an Oklahoma City PTA co-chairperson. As the evening reached its dismally unsatisfactory conclusion, Cassidy asked if she would now marry him.

"If it's all right with my husband," she said.

She must be Amish, I decided.

As I filed out of the theater that evening, gliding past a pair of newlyweds who had decided to spend their honeymoon in the company of the Last Partridge, I realized that I had spent more money to see David Cassidy than I had ever spent on a musical event in my entire life. I spent $40 or $50 to see the Rolling Stones, Herbert von Karajan, Van Morrison, Andrés Segovia. The most I ever shelled out to see Luciano Pavarotti or Placido Domingo was $67.50. Yet that night, I had forked over a cool seventy bucks to see Cassidy sing badly, dance badly, act badly, and get totally sandbagged by a women he dredged up from the audience.

It was worth every penny of it.

There was one other thing I noticed about Vegas.

At Excalibur, the knights had ponytails.

At Excalibur, the retainers had ponytails.

At the Mirage lounge, the musicians had ponytails.

On the streets of Vegas, the cabdrivers had ponytails.

Yet the whole time I was there, the ponytails didn't bother me.

I was even thinking about growing a ponytail of my own.

I was fading fast.

In the Monkees' first hit single, Mickey Dolenz sings the words: "Take the last train to Clarksville, and I'll meet you at the station." Implicit in the exhortation that someone take the last train to a locale where all that will be waiting for them is Mickey Dolenz—perhaps accompanied by Peter Tork—is the intimation, however vague, that the person is in fact leaving a place worse than Clarksville.

That place is Branson.

Branson, Missouri, is a cultural penal colony located in the northern Ozarks just a stone's throw from the Arkansas border. Just as Austria is really Germany, and Canada is really the United States, Branson, though technically located in the North, is truly in the South. Once the evil geniuses behind this Bayreuth for Bozos decided to create a major tourist attraction, it was imperative that the town be located in Missouri, because lots of people like my mother would have no problem visiting a town above the Mason-Dixon line but would hesitate to venture into Darkest Arkansas. Since southerners have spent so much of the past century talking about how much they hate Yankees, Yankees have learned to hate them back.

By reputation, Branson is known as a Bad Nashville, an elephant's graveyard for washed-up shitkickers. But in recent years, Branson has become a retirement home for has-beens of all stripes. Bobby Vinton has a theater there. Yakov Smirnoff has a theater there. Tony Orlando and Wayne Newton share a theater there. None of them are country-and-western stars.

Though the town first became a sort of Mulefuckers Mecca in 1967 when obscure groups with appropriate names like the Baldknobbers started to set up shop just outside the town proper, Modern Branson came into being in 1983 when aging Grand Old Opry fixture Roy Clark built a theater there. Since then, it has grown into a mammoth draw, luring more than 5 million people a year, none of them under seventy. When I visited Branson in the fall of 1997, the only people in town who were not collecting Social Security were Tony Orlando, Bobby Vinton, possibly Barbara Mandrell, and me.

Branson is as close to Hell as anything I have ever seen in my life. And I grew up in North Philadelphia. Basically, it is a loop of four or five thoroughfares on which are situated absolutely nothing but restaurants, motels, and theaters with huge parking lots to accommodate the gazillions of tour buses that empty out their geriatric cargo every afternoon. Because concerts are scheduled at 9:30 A.M., 11:00 A.M., 2:00 P.M., 3:00 P.M., 7:00 P.M., and 8:00 P.M., and are fairly cheap, it is possible to see as many as four events a day. Owing to a tight schedule back home, I could only spend two full days in Branson, but in that time I managed to see seven different shows. One day I heard the Lennon Brothers (the siblings of the Lennon Sisters), Mandrell, Tony Orlando (sans Dawn), and Branson's biggest star of all, a mop-topped, fiftyish Japanese fiddler named Shoji Tabuchi. This was a suckfest par excellence.

From the moment I arrived in Branson, I felt like Siegfried entering Valhalla. This was, at long last, the bottom of the pit. Here was Barbara Mandrell performing a rap version of "You Are My Sunshine," complete with gangsta sunglasses and black watchcap. Here was Tony Orlando frantically aborting a singalong version of the finale to "Hey, Jude" when he suddenly realized that I was the only other person in the room who knew the lyrics. The lyrics, for the record, are: "Na, na, na, na-na-na-na, na-na-na-na, hey, Jude."

And here were the Osmond Brothers, whose show is performed entirely on ice, with dogs, magic tricks, and jugglers, concluding their set by dangling a gigantic portrait of Our Lord and Savior and singing, "Till We Meet at Jesus' Feet." Presumably, when we meet at Jesus' feet, He, like everyone in the Osmond Brothers show, will be wearing ice skates.

Oh, there were memories enough for a lifetime! Tony Orlando sharing his dreams of making it to the top when he was a poor kid growing up in New York in the 1950s, and then realizing that he was now in Branson. And I honestly couldn't remember the last time I had seen a stand-up comic do a Jew joke, but the short, porcine comedian who opened for Barbara Mandrell actually used this material during his interminable set:

"A Jewish lady's husband died, so she called the newspaper to put in a funeral announcement.

'How much is it?' she asked.

'A dollar a word,' she was told.

'Print "Herb died,"' she said.

'There's a five-word minimum,' she was informed.

'Print "Herb Died; Car for Sale."'"

Let me say a few words about the kinds of people you tend to meet in Branson. Basically, you meet your uncle Bob and your aunt Clara. Decent people. Likable people. People who hold the door for you. The kind of people you wouldn't mind being stuck in a foxhole or a lifeboat with. You just wouldn't want to be stuck in a conversation with them.

All that said, this was a badly shod crowd. Particularly the men. When Tony Orlando's son, himself a gifted stand-up comic, invited the four funniest guys in the auditorium up on stage to tell their best jokes, I couldn't help noticing that Duane, Earl, Leon, and Woody were all wearing jeans and sneakers and the kinds of polo shirts your mommy dresses you in when you're four. Tony Orlando, by contrast, was in tails and top hat. It made you realize how far Tony had fallen. Here were four guys with the kinds of names none of my friends have, four guys with the kinds of names you wouldn't let anybody into your house, much less your life, with, and they were all wearing sneakers. It was a beautiful fall night, it was eight o'clock in the evening, their wives were all nicely turned out, Tony Orlando was in tails and top hat, the band looked scrubbed and spiffy, and these jokers were dressed in sneakers. They were all dressed like they'd just gone outside to clip a few vines with the Weed Whacker or to put out the cat.

Would it have been asking too much for these guys to feign a smidgen of interest and put on a nice pair of Dockers and some loafers? Under the best of circumstances, senior citizens look ridiculous in sneakers, but on this particular occasion—on a night when their wives and girlfriends and Tony Orlando were in the mood for moonlight and romance—how hard would it have been for them to show just a little bit of class? This has always been my one big complaint against my parents' generation: They won the Second World War and then figured that this gave them the right to dress badly for the next sixty years.

The most amazing thing about Branson is that it is the only place in the world that could possibly make you feel sorry for Tony Orlando. Branson is the place you go when it's over. Branson is the place you go when it's way over. In New York or Vegas, singers save their biggest hits for last. In Branson, "Moon River" is the first number Andy Williams performs, and Tony Orlando *opens* with "Tie a Yellow Ribbon Round the Ole Oak Tree," no doubt fearing that the audience will drift off or die before the second act. In Branson, people who already have one foot in the grave come to see performers who already have both. That's why the Lawrence Welk show is so popular. Lawrence Welk is only slightly deader than Tony Orlando.

Yet there will always be a soft spot in my heart for Branson, not because it sucked far beyond my wildest dreams of suckiness, but because it was here that my psychological rehabilitation finally began. Without Branson, I would not be here today. For it was in Branson that it finally hit home how far I had fallen from the state of grace.

Phase one of my regeneration began in the lobby of the Osmond Brothers Theater, where I stood after the concert had ended, gazing at the portraits adorning the walls. They were the kinds of tacky watercolors that usually commemorate weddings and bar mitzvahs, the kind of paintings where the smiles are always toothsome and the hair is always Fawcettian. There was Vicki Lawrence. There was Dionne Warwick. There was Tammy Faye Baker. And Paul Williams. And Dr. Joyce Brothers. And Hervé Villechaize. And Tim Conway. And David Hasselhoff. And Charo. And yes, there was Ricardo Montalban. My nightmare of a few months past had not been the stuff of fiction. It really was a conspiracy. And the evidence was right here, in the deepest recesses of the inner sanctum of the Star Chamber of the Temple of Doom of the Tri-Lateral Commission of Suck. Well, the foyer.

I went back to the hotel that night, deeply shaken by my experiences of the day. I, a man who owned all of Elvis Costello's records, a man who had seen David Byrne twice, a man who had given Brian Eno's *Music for Airports* as a Christmas present, a man who had seen Patti Smith in concert long before she was famous, a man who could spell "Twyla Tharp," a man who knew what the acronym BAM stood for, had just spent forty-five minutes in a chilly, crowded parking lot hoping to get an autograph or even a glimpse of one of the Osmond Brothers. How had I sunk this low? Was there no way out of this morass?

I tried to divert myself by reading James Clavell's *Shogun*. *Shogun* tells the tale of a hapless, pasty-faced Anglo-Saxon who falls into the hands of a merciless Japanese tyrant. (Tell me about it, Jimbo: I'd just spent the afternoon trapped in a room with Shoji Tabuchi, the Japanese Doug Kershaw.) I prayed for sleep. But sleep would not come. Sleep never came these days. I spent the entire night rolling around in bed, tantalized by images of Canadian Branson, a town that was a cross between ye olde Colonial Williamsburg and the hellhole where I currently found myself, where Bryan Adams had a theater, and Paul Anka had a theater, and Gordon Lightfoot had a theater, and Bachman-Turner Overdrive had a theater, and Joni Mitchell had a theater, and Anne Murray had a theater, and the Guess Who had a theater, and "Persons of the Past" dressed in flannel shirts like Neil Young walked around and said, "You can be in my dreams if I can be in yours, hey?"

The next day, I was confronted by one of those difficult choices that makes life such an infernal conundrum. At two o'clock I arrived at Bobby Vinton's baby blue, chateaulike theater and bought a ticket to the show. Incredibly, my seat was front-row center, right on the aisle. Bobby looked happy to see me. When he asked everyone where they were from, he asked me first. He shook my hand. Hey, why not? I was forty years younger than anyone else in the room, perhaps fifty. "Maybe," Bobby's expression seemed to suggest as I took my seat, "just maybe this career thing is starting to turn around. Maybe I'm starting to attract the youngsters with this material. Hey, Bobby Dylan still draws the kids."

Vinton's show was a peerless mix of his own Golden Oldies and the kind of paleolithic chestnuts the seniors go in for. In addition to such hits as "Blue Velvet," "Roses Are Red," "Blue on Blue," and other colorful numbers, Bobby, backed by the Glenn Miller Orchestra, his daughters, his mom, and his son (a bass player with full-blown ponytail) also performed "Chattanooga Choo-Choo," "In the Mood," "Beer Barrel Polka," and "God Bless America." This is one of the most noticeable things about the shows in Branson: Everybody does "In the Mood," everybody does "Beer Barrel Polka," everybody does "Chattanooga Choo-Choo," everybody does "Coming to America," and everybody ends their set with a patriotic medley. Thus, even though you attend three different shows each day, every show is pretty much the same. It's like masturbation: the *Sports Illustrated* swimsuit issue worked the first time, so why change the routine?

The single exception to this format was Andy Williams. Andy Williams doesn't really belong in Branson. He's too classy, too sophisticated, too polished. He's a young Perry Como. And Perry Como doesn't do poop jokes. Neither does Andy. Say what you will, but Andy Williams never, ever became a parody of himself. And yes, the cat still knows how to fill out a sweater. His gorgeous theater, all pastels, looks like a highly respected Holistic Health Center in Palos Verdes. I know, because when Bobby Vinton took a break at three o'clock, I bolted across the street to catch Andy, whose show began at three. It was a refined and well-paced program. Lush arrangements of "Hawaiian Wedding Song," "MacArthur Park," and, of course, "Moon River." Witty banter. A capable, energetic band. Frequent costume changes. And no schmaltz whatsoever.

Alas, as was so often the case, schmaltz was what I was on the prowl for. And even though I desperately wanted to hear my Huckleberry Friend sing "Almost There," "The Impossible Dream," and the "Love Theme from the *Godfather*,"

I looked at my watch and realized that Vinton's show was now into its second act, and that if I didn't rush back across Highway 76 I'd never get to hear Bobby Vinton sing "My Melody of Love." Let's face it: You don't come all the way from New York to Branson and not get to hear Bobby Vinton sing "My Melody of Love." It would be like going to the Vatican and not getting to see the Pietà.

So I bolted out of the theater. I hauled ass across the parking lot. I looked both ways. And then I ran into the middle of the highway. But as I arrived at the median strip, I was jolted by an electric shock. This was the defining moment of my entire sojourn on this planet. One part of me, the Old Joe Queenan, implored me to turn tail and go back to hear Andy Williams sing the tasteful, elegant "Days of Wine and Roses." The other part of me, the dark side, the Edward Hyde portion of my personality that had fallen under Geraldo Rivera's malefic sway, commanded me to go forward and hear Bobby Vinton sing in Polish.

Suddenly, a truck loomed up a few feet to my left. Miraculously, I saw the truck in time to jump out of the way. But, like Saul on the road to Damascus, I had glimpsed the Valley of Death. I now saw myself for what I was: a middle-aged man who had once fancied himself a paragon of culture and sophistication, who was marooned on a median strip in Hades-by-the-Ozarks, torn between Bobby Vinton and Andy Williams.

But unlike Saul of Tarsus, I did not answer God's call when He knocked me from my horse with a blazing bolt of lightning. Saul changed his name to Paul and chose the Way of Christ.

I chose the Way of Vinton.

Deliverance

Met the dancing lady in the high summer of '66 in the high plains of North Dakota when the wind was far and good and true. Waltzed across the Panhandle, traveling light and fast, singing Mexican songs that hadn't yet been written about the high, misty places where the chaparral wrapped its tendrils around the cedar. Dreamed of moving to the big city, maybe landing a job at *GQ*. Never happened—too much of a drifter, a loner, a maverick, a cowboy dreaming of the high, true, far places where the dancing ladies tell you the secrets only the *viejos* know.

Actually, none of this ever happened. I have never been to North Dakota, have never visited the Panhandle, and wouldn't know the high, true, far places if one of them bit me on the ass. It was just that after months and months of reading books like *Border Music*, *Slow Waltz in Cedar Bend*, *Old Songs in a New Café*, *Puerto Vallarta Squeeze*, and, of course, *The Bridges of Madison County*, I was starting to write like that knucklehead Robert James Waller.

This was not the first time that this sort of thing had

happened to me, but obviously it was the most serious. As touched upon in an earlier chapter, the worst thing about my addiction was its effect on my work as a journalist. For years I had been writing book reviews for *The New York Times*, *The Wall Street Journal*, *Barron's*, and *The American Spectator*, but earlier in the spring I had informed my editors that I was only interested in reviewing books that stunk beyond belief. My editors were most accommodating, sending me Sarah Ferguson's lunkheaded autobiography, Marcia Clark's sad attempt to explain how she lost the least losable murder case in American history, and Mia Farrow's addled account of her life with the Man of Wood.

But the events of recent months had rendered me incapable of handling even these assignments! Part of it was the *stress*. But some of it was the *subtle but pronounced* influence my psychological disability was exerting *on my* writing style!!! Every time I tried to do *my work*, the cumulative effect of reading so many Robert Ludlum books caused me to end every sentence with an exclamation point!!!! And *when that didn't happen*, the similar fallout from gorging on Stephen King *forced me to include italics* to describe even *the* most mundane *of* events!!!!

And when you start writing stuff like that, editors stop calling.

I am the only person I know who has read the complete works of Robert James Waller. It is a distinction of which I am not proud. But at least it has taught me new ways to insult the man. Long before I embarked on my Marco Polo– like caravan to the Walled City of Suck, other critics far more gifted than I had taken the hammer to this Great Plains Flaubert, pointing out his obvious debts to John Steinbeck, Ernest Hemingway, and Spot. To these insights, let me add only this: Critics are badly mistaken if they think *The Bridges of Madison County* is Waller's worst creation. *Puerto Vallarta Squeeze* is a million times worse than the novel that made Waller famous. *Slow Waltz in Cedar Bend* is 10 million times worse. *The Songs of the Bridges of Madison County* is 300 billion times worse. But none of these moronic titles even approaches the high-adrenaline idiocy of *Border Music*. No one will ever write a book worse than *Border Music*. The government wouldn't allow it.

But this is not the worst charge that can be leveled at the high plains nitwit. One day toward the end of my journey, I dug into my dwindling reserves of unadulterated garbage and dredged up *Smokey and the Bandit*. This is the 1977 film in which Burt Reynolds plays a man who drives a fast car across the rural South on assorted two-lane blacktops. Mixing myself a rich Suck Cocktail, I also turned on Rush Limbaugh, logged onto a brain-dead chat room on the Internet, heated up an ominous-looking TV dinner, and read the last few chapters of *Border Music*. While doing so, I made a stunning discovery.

Border Music, published in 1993, was a complete rip-off of *Smokey and the Bandit*. *Smokey* tells the tale of a no-account drifter. *Border Music* tells the tale of a no-account drifter. *Smokey* is set in the South. *Border Music* is set in the South. *Smokey* is about a maverick who puts down no roots and likes to listen to shitkicker's music. *Border Music* is about a maverick who puts down no roots and likes to listen to shitkicker's music. In *Smokey*, Burt Reynolds falls in love with a woman he meets while rolling down that long, lonesome highway. In *Border Music*, Jack Carmine falls in love with a woman he meets while rolling down that long, lonesome highway. In *Smokey*, the hero's name is Bandit. In *Border Music*, Jack Carmine's nickname is Bandit. Thus, just as *The Bridges of Madison County* was a blatant rip-off, a cornshuck *Madame Bovary,* if you will, *Border Music* was a complete rip-off of *Smokey and the Bandit.* Proving that Robert James Waller was the biggest dunce in the history of American letters.

Being in possession of this information did me no good whatsoever. With Waller's entire oeuvre under my belt, I literally had none of the all-time bad books left to read. Like a Long Knife pinned down by the Kiowa, I was now forced to make every bullet count. And my movie bandolier was running low, too. I had seen every Eric Roberts movie ever made. I had rented *Mary Reilly, Encino Man, Xanadu.* I had seen all three *Oh, God!* pictures. Yet, by this point, predictably, many of the bad movies that I had been count-ing on to nutritionally sustain me until I could find a cure turned out to be woefully unbad. *The Evil Dead II* was entirely watchable. So was *The Milagro Beanfield War.* Oh why, oh why, hadn't they ever made a sequel to *Red Sonja?*

From the moment that truck narrowly missed hitting me in Branson, I knew that the countdown to oblivion had begun. So did everyone else, who urged me to go for broke in my search for a magic bullet. My family and friends didn't care if I lost my mind in my Burton/Speke–like trek to the source of the Neanderthal Nile, but losing my life was a whole other kettle of fish. Maybe it was time for psy-chological counseling, they opined. Maybe it was time to be institutionalized. Maybe it was time for hypnosis. Or electroshock therapy.

Luckily for me, it never came to that. Mercifully, sal-vation was nigh. Yes, I prayed. I prayed to St. Jude, the patron saint of lost causes. I prayed to St. Joseph, my name-sake. I even prayed to St. Bernadette. In French. After all, the French thought Jerry Lewis was a genius, so maybe they'd give me a break for going to see him in *Damn Yankees*.

Were my prayers answered? Yes, but my deliverance from the hands of mine enemy occurred in a most unlikely fashion. One morning I was watching the next-to-last movie on my list of personal horror shows. *The Blue Lagoon* is the film where Leo McKern is shipwrecked on a desert island with two youngsters played by Elva Josephson and Glenn Kohan. One day he swims to a nearby island to die, determined to flee the movie before the child actors get a chance to turn into Brooke Shields and Christopher Atkins. Now the children are even worse off than before: trapped on an island where no one can cook in a film where no one can act. Call it *Swiss Family Shields*.

That same morning, I picked up a copy of *Kevorkian Suite: A Very Still Life*. This was a jazz CD that had recently been released by Dr. Death himself. Four dollars out of the purchase of each CD would help finance the construction of a "patholysis clinic" meant to be a "safe haven" for people who want to pull the plug in a dignified setting. I wanted that CD. I loved that CD. But more to the point, I wanted Kevorkian to build that patholysis clinic as soon as possible. I'd seen Kenny G, Liza Minnelli, and John Tesh live and on stage within scant weeks of each other. I was ready to go.

The final ingredient in my matinal Suck Cocktail was Michael Crichton's *The Andromeda Strain*. This was the twenty-eight-year-old thriller about a virus so deadly that it killed healthy human beings as soon as they took a breath. Much of the book dealt with the desperate attempts by a group of fugitive scientists to develop something that could kill off the virus.

Hey, wait a minute! What if I had a virus? What if this

whole nightmare was the result of fiendish microbes invading my nervous system and compelling me to listen to Billy Joel's entire catalog? And what if I turned the tables on the virus by developing an antivirus?

Think, Joe, think! When had this whole process of mental deterioration begun? When I'd shaken hands with Geraldo Rivera? When I'd developed a mysterious affection for Barry Manilow? Or did it go back even farther? Had the virus entered my system months and months earlier, and then only gradually, imperceptibly begun to take control of my personality? Was it possible that the virus had been there right from the beginning of my experiment? And if so, where had the virus been concealed?

Frantically, I wracked my brain. Had I caught the infection on my visit to Atlantic City, perhaps due to deadly microorganisms lurking in the water? Or had it entered my nervous system through my auditory nerves when I'd first put Michael Bolton's *Classics* on the CD player? Or had the real culprit been cunningly concealed in the Admiral's Feast at Red Lobster?

And then I saw the big picture. It was obvious how this whole thing had gotten started. I had launched myself on this perilous adventure by willingly subjecting myself to the worst cultural experience on this entire planet. For months upon months I had struggled valiantly to find other experiences of equal or surpassing wretchedness. But throughout that long, dark night of the soul, nothing had quite matched that first event for epic unpleasantness. Tesh had come close. Robert James Waller was in the ballpark. Branson was certainly a worthy contender. But in the end, in each and every instance, it had been close, but no cigar.

The path lay clear. It was time to go back and reexpose myself to the malignancy that had brought me to my knees.

Like a high plains drifter bitten by a rattlesnake in the far, true places where the wind comes ripping 'cross the high plains where I was drifting, I knew that the only antidote to the rattler's venom was the rattler's venom itself.

It was time to go back to see *Cats*.

When they talk about *Cats: Now and Forever!*—they're not just talking about the show itself. When I arrived for the Saturday afternoon matinee of the lethal musical, I could have sworn that it was the same crowd with whom I had reluctantly commingled eighteen months earlier. The same phalanxes of remorseless Japanese tourists. The same squadrons of Linda-Blair-in-*Roller-Boogie* impersonators with Five Towns Hair. The same Legion of Doom numbskulls who've been out of the loop since Day One.

I was not entirely sure what I was expecting that day. I couldn't decide whether I was hoping for some sort of cinematic miracle during the course of which I would toss away my crutches and walk, or something much more subtle— like a secret hand signal from one of the cats. I only knew that if this gambit didn't work, my life wasn't worth a brass farthing.

Looking back on that October afternoon, I can recall that shortly before the theater went dark, one part of me hoped that the lights would never dim. For who knew what lay ahead—salvation or perdition? Especially with my luck. Like a condemned man standing at the foot of the gallows, I wanted to savor those last few moments before Death wrapped its icy mantle around my shivering carcass, before Mother Night engulfed me forever.

As I sat in the balcony waiting for *Cats* to begin, I realized that there could be no moment during my sojourn on this planet more precious than the seconds immediately preceding this curtain-raising. The emotions I was experiencing were much like those that Adam and Eve must have felt, wondering what was coming next as the Gates of Heaven closed behind them for all eternity.

On the other hand, all Adam and Eve had to deal with when they left the Garden of Eden was Satan. I still had to deal with Andrew Lloyd Webber.

The lights did finally dim, and the show was ready to begin. The crowd settled in, the first god-awful notes sounded, the musical began. The cats slithered onto the stage, prowling, hissing. I knew them well! There was Munkustrap. And Mistoffelees. There lurked Bombalurina, and, not far away, Mungojerrie. Yes, the Jellicle Ball was in full swing. As the king-sized felines crept around the stage, I noted that they still looked very much like KISS. The original KISS. Long in the tooth. Frazzled. Resigned to their fate, yet convinced that with a few breaks here and there, they could have been Van Halen. As for the story, well, I still couldn't figure out what the story was about. And the music still sounded like the stuff you hear on "Starsky and Hutch" when they have to chase some child molester.

A cat appeared on the railing a few feet in front of me. Was it Rumpleteazer? Or the Rum Tum Tugger? It was hard to tell; he was facing the stage. He was wagging his tail, not always a good thing for a man in shiny tights to do in New York City. I watched him slither across the railing, hoping that he'd fall off and kill a couple of Japanese tourists down below. That way the management would have to stop the show and give everyone a refund before skanky old Grizabella could come out and sing "Memory." Jesus, I thought, what a bunch of strange coincidences. Grizabella sang "Memory."

Barry Manilow sang "Memory." Shoji Tabuchi played "The Music of the Night," which had been composed by the man who wrote "Memory." So did Bobby Vinton, who also sang "Chattanooga Choo-Choo," as did the Osmonds, as well as Barry Manilow, whose last big hit was "Memory," which was the song I wouldn't have to hear today if that cat on the railing lost his footing, fell, and killed a couple of tourists who had flown here from the same country as Shoji Tabuchi.

And then, I saw the light.

My mind was wandering. My mind was thinking about other things. And there was a good reason for this. Like the man who had first set foot in this theater eighteen months ago, expecting the worst, I didn't want to think about what was taking place right before my very eyes. Mentally, now as then, my mind was elsewhere.

Why?

Because I hated this show.

I mean *hated* it. I don't mean that I hated it so much that I liked it. I mean that I just plain hated it. I hated the songs. I hated the costumes. I hated the sets. I hated the performers. I hated the audience. I hated the building. I hated the primordial forces in the universe that tolerated, and even encouraged, this kind of situation.

Most of all, I hated the fact that I was there.

This was nothing like the sensation I'd been experiencing in recent months, like the adrenaline rush of Bransonian suckiness that had given me a brief high. This was pure pain. This was sheer torture. *Cats* really was the worst thing on the entire planet. Which, considering the planet's overall record in this area, was quite a statement. This was suffering, and I didn't want to suffer anymore. What's more, I didn't *have* to suffer anymore.

To this day, I'm not certain what transpired in that particular moment in that particular circle of hell. Perhaps some awesome neurobiological phenomenon seized control of my body, sending shock waves through my neuropeptide reservoirs. Perhaps the psychic substratum of my being underwent some inexplicable, submolecular volcanic activity. Or perhaps I had just read too many books by Tony Robbins and Deepak Chopra. In any case, it didn't matter. Somehow, some way, the twin curses of Andrew Lloyd Webber and Geraldo Rivera had been lifted.

At long last, the fever had broken.

★   ★   ★

As I look back on my experiences, I am aware that at a certain point my ordeal began to take on messianic overtones. Just as Jesus had taken on the sins of the world in order that the Gates of Heaven might be reopened, I had taken on the sins of the world so that no one else would have to see Tony Orlando and the Osmonds the same evening. Lots of people have seen *Victor/Victoria*, lunched at Red Lobster, read Danielle Steel, dined at the Olive Garden, and listened to three Michael Bolton CDs. But how many have done it all in the same day, and then gotten up and done it again and again every day for months on end? This is why, in the end, I feel justified in comparing my eighteen months of bondage to the fourteen Stations of the Cross or even to the horrifying Sun Dance ritual that Richard Harris had to endure in *A Man Called Horse* in order to prove his manhood to a tribe of highly dysfunctional aboriginals. Believe me, things that you wouldn't want to do once, I've done not only twice but, in some cases, thrice.

What, in the end, did I learn from my long voyage on the Sea of Poop? Sadly, not a whole lot. Like Odysseus, absent twenty years from his native land, I learned that I would have been a whole lot better off if I'd stayed at home.

I learned that there are places man was never meant to go, like Radio City Music Hall any night Kenny G is playing there. But this was not something I hadn't known before.

I learned that there are recesses in the human heart where nothing exists, so Evil takes up residence. But you didn't have to read Stephen King to know that.

The only thing of lasting value I had learned at the end of my ordeal was to stop taking what I had for granted. Yes, it was sad to live in a world where Garth Brooks, and not Dwight Yoakam, sold more records than Elvis and got to perform concerts in Central Park. But in a truly evil world, there wouldn't have even been a Dwight Yoakam or an Elvis. And Garth Brooks would have been playing at La Scala.

In the nineteenth century, when civilized men went in search of the heart of darkness, they traveled to Africa. In the late twentieth century, they go to Branson. But nobody ever said that those men *had to go* to the Dark Continent. And nobody ever said that I had to go to southern Missouri. I went because it was there. But there are lots of places that are *there*. It doesn't mean you have to visit them.

My readjustment to normal life has not been easy. To this day, some of my friends chide me for the many spectacularly hideous diversions that I neglected in my crusade. They feel that it was a mistake to miss Tony Danza singing and dancing at the Rainbow Room. And why hadn't I jumped on a train and caught Phil Collins on the next leg of his tour after his final Madison Square Garden show was canceled in March? And what self-respecting connoisseur of sludge could bring himself to admit that he has never seen *The Texas Chainsaw Massacre*, the very last comestible in my larder of odious foodstuffs?

From my point of view, this was sheer nitpicking. True, I hadn't done every horrendous thing that a person could do in the time span allotted me, but I'd come pretty damn close. Yet weeks after the ordeal had ended, I continued to receive hot tips from friends who had not heard of my cure. One do-gooder informed me that the Smothers Brothers would be playing a Thursday, October 17, concert at the Foxwoods Casino in northern Connecticut. A month earlier, I would have leaped at the chance to see such a hair-raising show. Now I simply went to the bus stop, watched the pilgrims clamber aboard, and whispered: "There but for the grace of God go I."

An important lesson I gleaned from my descent into Hell is that it is possible to live in a world of schlock without collapsing under its sheer mass. John Tesh, like diphtheria, will always exist; you just have to stay indoors when he is sighted in the district. Obviously, the fear of a relapse is something I worry about every day of my life. But I have profited from my bitter experiences in France last summer. I have learned to call for my check and leave quietly whenever I find myself in a restaurant where the pianist seems poised to play "Feelings" or "Your Song." I have learned to avoid what Mother Church refers to as *the proximate occasions of sin*. Like a smoker who has kicked the habit, I do not feel the need to steal an occasional smoke to see if my recovery is permanent. I am taking no chances. I am never watching the tape of Garth Brooks's Central Park concert. Never.

Only once since my rebirth did I deviate from this rule. Scant weeks after I, Lazarus-like, emerged from *Cats*, I found myself in Sydney, Australia, where I had been invited to give a speech sponsored by the Australian Film Institute. The day before the speech, I was interviewed by a young journalist from the *Sydney Morning Herald.* The interview was supposed to take place in my hotel room overlooking Sydney's gorgeous harbor, but at the last moment, the AFI publicist informed me that the venue had been changed. The new venue was Planet Hollywood.

Throughout my ordeal, I had not visited Planet Hollywood. It was one of just seven deadly sins on my internal checklist of unspeakable horrors that I had never checked off. I never went on a Caribbean cruise. I never became an Amway representative. I never watched *The Texas Chainsaw Massacre.* I never did the macarena. I never finished reading *Dune.* And I never grew a ponytail. Barring that return visit to *Cats,* I would probably have done all of these things in the fullness of time, very possibly the next day. Mercifully, I was spared these ignominies.

When I arrived at Planet Hollywood, my instinctive reaction was to run and hide. But that would have been unprofessional. I had a job to do; I was going to do it.

It was hard to get into the restaurant that day, because a throng of well wishers and media types had gathered for a Jon Bon Jovi press conference. I earnestly hoped that I would be turned away. I was not. Eventually, after a bit of hemming and hawing, the Steven Seagal types at Planet Hollywood let us in.

Planet Hollywood was as I expected it to be: totally unnecessary and very loud. Here hung Sylvester Stallone's robe from one of the *Rocky* films. There hung Demi Moore's autograph. And there, just a few inches away, hung Billy Baldwin's autograph. Not Alec Baldwin's.

Billy's.

I think that said it all.

Relieved by my visceral reaction to the establishment— it blew it out the ass and I couldn't wait to lift anchor—I sat down with the journalist and the interview began. I ordered a humongous brownie, foolishly started eating it, and answered a handful of questions about the current state of the American film industry. At no point did I feel enticed back into my former madness. I simply wanted to haul my ass out of there.

About five minutes into the interview, the AFI publicist appeared at my side.

"We have to leave," she informed me tersely.

"But we've only just started the interview."

"We have to leave," she repeated. *"There's been a bomb threat and they're vacating the building."*

I don't need to tell you how profoundly ironic it would have been had I, a survivor of the cultural equivalent of the Bataan Death March, been killed in an explosion at a Planet Hollywood the day Jon Bon Jovi was holding a press conference there. I don't need to tell you what compelling proof that would have provided that the universe, long thought to be indifferent, was actually downright mean. And I don't need to tell you how quickly I got the hell out of that building.

Since that afternoon, I've thought a lot about that incident. And what I've decided is this: The bomb scare wasn't a strange coincidence, a random event in a world without meaning. The bomb scare, with its deeply symbolic Bon Jovian symbolism, was a sign from God. *It was I who divulged the secret of* Cats *to you*, the Lord was saying, perhaps because St. Bernadette had passed along my request. *It was I who showed you the path out of the wilderness. It was I who led you to the Promised Land, or Tarrytown, New York, or wherever the hell it is you live. The first time that I punished you for your arrogance, I smote you with a flood.*

The fire next time.

INDEX

ABBA
  alarming popularity in
    Lourdes of, 137
Abelard, Peter
  one-size-fits-all letter to fans
    of, 27–28
  tragic surgical history of, 28
Adam and Eve
  lack of exposure to work of
    Andrew Lloyd Webber,
    182
AIDS
  plot device in vampire novel,
    36
  Whoopi's concern about, 83
Alexander the Great
  as more durable role model
    than Lee Iacocca or Pete
    Rose, 150
Aykroyd, Dan
  capriciously insulted, 42

  capriciously insulted, 48
  when coupled with
    "Starring," two scariest
    words in English
    language, 10

Bergman, Sandahl
  paleolithically skimpy
    costumes of, 44
Bernadette, Saint
  and Kenny G, 137
Blair, Linda
  influence of *Roller Boogie*
    hair on *Cats* audiences,
    181
Bolton, Michael
  ability to make "Yesterday"
    actually sound worse than
    the original, 8
  federal offenses of, 8
  likened to ebola virus, 7–8

Branson, Missouri
  as cultural penal colony,
    166
Brooks, Garth
  likens "old highway" to "a
    woman," 14
  not terribly big in France,
    134
  and Red Hot Chili Peppers,
    15
  suspected of being Glen
    Campbell under an
    assumed name, 14
Butterfly, Iron
  no real improvement on
    Liberace, 1

Canadian Branson
  as retirement home for
    Gordon Lightfoot, Anne
    Murray, Bryan Adams,
    Paul Anka, and the Guess
    Who, 171
Cannonball Run II
  hat of author taken off to,
    50–52
  influence of Amiens
    Cathedral on, 130
Cartel, Cali
  tonsorial influences on bass
    players in Freddy Roman's
    band, 19
Carter, Jimmy
  gratuitously insulted, 98
  poetry questioned, 120
  prime interest rates and,
    120

refusal of American people
    to admit they voted for
    him, 54
Cassidy, David
  hootiness of, 163–165
Cats
  similarity of score to theme
    from *Mod Squad*, 6
  stunning appeal to gawking
    midwestern huckleberries,
    7
Chopra, Deepak
  ability to keep straight face
    while saying that that
    which the seeker was
    seeking was the seeker
    and having sought the
    seeker, it has become the
    seer, 153
Clancy, Tom
  delineates antitorture
    techniques that can be
    used to survive a
    performance of *Grease*,
    100
  made fun of for no good
    reason, 142
Cleveland
  best tiramisu of, 90
Collins, Jackie
  even worse than sister Joan,
    29
Collins, Joan
  command of sixth-grade
    French of, 29
  and stone steps that crumble
    like Camembert, 32

Collins, Phil
  undeniable existence of, 66–
    67
Collins, Tom
  fourth leg of weak joke
    about bad things that end
    in the word "Collins," 104
Cosell, Howard
  belated realization that
    absolutely everyone hated
    his guts, 76
Cranberries, the
  compared to the Raspberries,
    88

Danza, Tony
  forming common threat with
    Tony Orlando, 2
  indelible regrets of author
    regarding, 185
Davis, Jr., Sammy
  unforgivable crimes of, 74
Delibes, Leo
  influence on Yanni, 141
Diamond, Neil
  hard rockin' tonight of, 13
  longin' for country roads of,
    13
  serious attempt to relocate
    that girl Annie, 13
Donahue, Phil
  hubris of, 23
  likened to Ozymandias, 23

Episcopalianism
  seriousness of denomination

called into question, 147–
    48

Fawcett, Farrah
  grooming influence on *Cats*
    audiences of, 7
  grooming influence on the
    Branson, Missouri, crowd,
    170
French, the
  Broadway patrons' puzzling
    affection for in *Les
    Miserables*, 94
  occasional usefulness of, 127–
    28
  typical failure to come
    through in the clutch of,
    137

G, Kenny
  Blessed Virgin Mary
    unimpressed by work of,
    137
  Electric Light Orchestra hair
    of, 67
  theoretical liaison with
    Messrs. Rogers and
    Loggins, 69
Garden, Olive
  influence of Chef Boyardee
    on menu, 106
  zuppa toscana of, 107
Goya, Francisco de
  inability to prevent Stephen
    King from using his
    material in *The Shining* to

make the book seem less
idiotic, 28
Greene, Shecky
not really all that much worse
than Iron Butterfly, 1

Hitler, Adolf
compared to Mare
Winningham, 53
musical tastes likened to
John Tesh's, 78

Incas
as pathetic losers, 12

Joel, Billy
entire career called into
question, 63–67
Jovi, Jon Bon
and Australian bomb scare,
187–88
facial similarity to characters
in *Cats* of, 6
Jude, Saint
refusal to help author in
hour of need, 178

King, Stephen
fascination with auricular
trauma, 36
Kings, Gipsy
as ethnic ABBA, 146

Leo I, Pope
and Joe Pesci, 42
turning away Attila the Hun
at the gates of Rome,
42

Letterman, David
as proof of Western
Civilization's vast
superiority to a culture
that produced Deepak
Chopra and Ravi Shankar,
154
Lewis, Jerry
author's daughter baffled by
appeal of, 73
Lobster, Red
children's tragic inability to
detect lack of point of,
104
snootiness of sad-sack
clientele, 10
troubling appeal to
contemporary
"landlubbers," 11
Lourdes
as French Niagara Falls, 135

MacGraw, Ali
suspected witchcraft of, 59
Madison County
the bridges of, 175–77
Manilow, Barry
likened to Jerry Lewis and
Sammy Davis, Jr., 72
schmaltziness of, 74
Mead
best when drunk from
flagon, 125
Minnelli, Liza
author's daughter baffled by
appeal of, 105
Montalban, Ricardo
insulted, 51

insulted, 146
no worse than David
    Cassidy, 164
Moore, Demi
    alphabetical listing in most
        terrifying cast of
        characters ever, 53
    implausible career of, 45
Moyers, Bill
    refusal to come to the point
        of, 151
    same old crap of, 153
Musburger, Brent
    as unspeakable horror
        lurking in the attic, 38

Newton, Wayne
    awareness that once you get
        started, it's too late to stop
        now, 162
    banjo solo on "Waitin' on
        the Robert E. Lee" of, 162
    cuff popping of, 162

Orlando, Tony
    failure to enlist geriatric
        audience in "Hey, Jude"
        singalong, 167
    needlessly hammered, 184
Osmond Brothers
    gathering at the feet of
        Jesus, 167–68
    and ice, 167

Pesci, Joe
    life being too short and
        precious to watch movies
        of, 40

Polloi, Hoi
    author's troubled
        relationship with, 3
Pot, Pol
    seeks to make amends for
        past indiscretions, 114
POW-MIA jackets
    inadvisability of small
        children accepting candy,
        doughnuts, or rides from
        middle-aged men clad in,
        103

Raspberries, the
    compared to the
        Cranberries, 88
Reynolds, Burt
    jaunty yarmulke of, 46
    star of last great bad movie,
        50–52
Ringwald, Molly
    America's refusal to deal
        with sinister legacy of, 54
Rivera, Geraldo
    inadvisability of shaking
        hands with, 113–16
    likened to Pol Pot, 114
    relationship with forces of
        primordial darkness, 50
Riverdance
    as Celtic hopscotch, 75

Saigon, Miss
    vastly overrated helicopter
        landing of, 96
Sandler, Adam
    and Black Death, 10
    as latter-day Ostrogoth, 9

Seinfeld, Jerry
  influence of pirate shirt on
    Michael Flatley, 75
Shakespeare, William
  blurbed by Tom Clancy, 29
Soccer
  obvious foolhardiness of,
    103
South, the
  entire hilarious chapter cut
    out of book by
    domineering editor
Stone, Oliver
  tendency to cinematically
    lionize assholes named
    Jim, 58
Streisand, Barbra
  as highly placed official in
    BOZO (Benign Order of
    Zenophobic Oligopolists),
    143
Swayze, Patrick
  as linchpin of anticloning
    argument, 84

Tesh, John
  Cornhusker Flamenco of,
    78
  hepness of, 75
  likened to Adolf Hitler, 78
  likened to diphtheria, 186
  obliviousness of, 76
  questionable goatee of, 78
Tharp, Twyla
  author's ability to spell name
    of as proof of awesome
    sophistication, 170

Titanic
  predictable finale of, 97

Villa, Pancho
  failure to prevent rise of
    Taco Bell, 123
Vinton, Bobby
  blueness of velvet of, 172
  redness of roses of, 172
  and Saul of Tarsus, 173

Waller, Robert James
  influence of Ernest
    Hemingway on, 176
  influence of Gustave
    Flaubert on, 176
  influence of John Steinbeck
    on, 176
  influence of *Smokey and the
    Bandit* on, 177–78
Welch, Raquel
  striking resemblance to
    Leona Helmsley of, 121
Wenches
  putative comeliness of, 124
Witchy Woman diet
  as component of novel but
    ineffective weight-loss
    program, 62

Yanni
  SAT scores of long-time fans
    called into question, 75
Yentl
  used as crude running joke,
    43–44
Yeomen
  stoutness of, 124